U-Boat Commander

FORTUNES OF WAR

U-BOAT COMMANDER

Günther Prien

TEMPUS

PUBLISHED IN THE UNITED KINGDOM BY:

Tempus Publishing Ltd

The Mill, Brimscombe Port

Stroud, Gloucestershire GL5 2QG

PUBLISHED IN THE UNITED STATES OF AMERICA BY:

Tempus Publishing Inc.

2 Cumberland Street

Charleston, SC 29401

Tempus books are available in France, Germany and Belgium
from the following addresses:

Tempus Publishing Group	Tempus Publishing Group	Tempus Publishing Group
21 Avenue de la République	Gustav-Adolf-Straße 3	Place de L'Alma 4/5
37300 Joué-lès-Tours	99084 Erfurt	1200 Brussels
FRANCE	GERMANY	BELGIUM

© Tempus Publishing

British Library Cataloguing in Publication Data.
A catalogue record for this book is available from the British Library.

ISBN 0 7524 2025 9

Typesetting and origination by Tempus Publishing.
PRINTED AND BOUND IN GREAT BRITAIN.

Contents

Hansard, 17 October 1939
U-Boat Warfare

In answer to a question by Mr A.V. Alexander, the First Lord of the Admiralty (Mr Winston Churchill) said: 'The battleship *Royal Oak* was sunk at anchor by a U-Boat in Scapa Flow at approximately 1.30 a.m. on the 14th instant. It is still a matter of conjecture how the U-Boat penetrated the defences of the harbour. When we consider that during the whole course of the last war, the anchorage was found to be immune from such attack, on account of the obstacles imposed by the currents and the net barrages, *this entry by a U-Boat must be considered as remarkable exploit of professional skill and daring.* A board of Inquiry is now sitting at Scapa Flow to report on all that occurred, and anything I say must be subject to revision in the light of their conclusions. It seems probable that the U-Boat fired a salvo of torpedoes at the *Royal Oak*, of which only one hit the bow. This muffled explosion was at the time attributed to internal causes, and what is called the inflammable store, where the kerosene and other such are kept, was flooded. Twenty minutes later the U-Boat fired 3 or 4 torpedoes, and these striking in quick succession caused the ship to capsize and sink. She was lying at the extreme end of the harbour and, therefore, many officers and men were drowned before rescue could be organised from other vessels. The list of survivors has already been made public, and I deeply regret to inform the House that upwards of 800 officers and men have lost their lives.'

One
The Start

It was in Leipzig in the evil summer of 1923: the inflation ruined us all. Our parents had become poor. The streets we were walking through were grey, dirty and unswept.

It was raining.

'Shall we tell 'em today?' asked Heinz.

I thought of my mother.

'I guess my old man will have a stroke,' Heinz said brightly. The prospect of paternal chastisement left him unmoved. He smacked himself in a significant gesture. He was as hard in giving as he was in taking.

We parted in front of my street door. After a few steps Heinz turned and called, 'I shall tell my old man today without fail.' Waving his satchel he disappeared round the corner.

I walked up the narrow wooden staircase, its worn steps were sparsely illuminated by small windows overlooking the courtyard. We were living on the second floor.

My mother opened the door. She wore her painting-smock.

'Pst, keep quiet Günther,' she whispered. 'Mr Buzelius is still asleep.'

He was the fat student who had the room by the front door. He had already been studying for seven years. He stayed in bed until noon. He said he could work best lying down. The door rattled with his snores.

I went into the back room. The table was already laid.

Liese Lotte and Hans Joachim sat on their high stools pale and timid. On the mantelpiece lay three letters in blue envelopes – bills!

My mother came into the room with the meal. It was barley soup. We ate in silence.

'Is it a lot?' I asked nodding towards the blue envelopes.

'The worst is the dentist's,' she sighed and added, 'People who have nothing to bite don't really need teeth.'

I looked at her. There was a bitter look on her good-natured round face. No, I couldn't tell her; at least, not then.

While she was clearing the table she said: 'When you have finished your homework take the lace to Kleewitz and Bramfeld; another boxful has arrived.'

I nodded. It was not a very exacting job, but at least we lived on it. My aunt bought the lace in the Erzgebirge; my mother sold it in Leipzig to small shops and to private customers. There was a meagre profit, and sometimes none.

I didn't go until evening. The box was unpleasantly large and I disliked being seen with it by my school friends. The shop was in the *Neumarkt,* a small shop with a tiny window displaying old-fashioned underwear and nightgowns with embroidery, little d'oyleys and pillow lace. It looked just as if a clothes basket of the 1880s had been emptied into the window.

The elder sister Kleewitz, a small dried up woman with a pointed nose and black eyes, was in the shop.

'Good evening,' I said, putting the box on the plate glass of the counter. 'I have brought the lace, from my mother.'

'You couldn't have come sooner, could you?' she said querulously. 'It's dark now.' She took the lid off the box and began to dig around in the lace muttering, 'Of course, unbleached again…and always the same pattern…"God's eyes," always "God's eyes"…Not a soul wants "God's eyes" nowadays…I told you that the last time.'

I said nothing.

The street door-bell rang and a customer came in.

Miss Kleewitz left me standing and went to serve her. It was fascinating to see how pleasant her face became and to hear how melting her voice sounded as she talked to her customer.

I stood there and watched it all. Yes, that was how they were, those miserable shopkeepers, servility for those above them and kicks for those below.

The customer walked off with a packet of pins. Miss Kleewitz returned to my box and scratched about in it like a hen digging for worms, murmuring again: 'The patterns were quite different…much prettier…and much more carefully worked…I hardly like to take this rubbish.'

'Well then…' I started.

She raised her head and looked at me. Her eyes narrowed to slits and her mouth gaped open. Another word from me and she would chuck me out, lace and all. I knew that as surely as if she had said so. I thought of my mother, the young ones at home, and kept silent.

'Did you say anything?' she asked.

'No.'

'Well, I wouldn't like to have heard anything anyhow,' she said triumphantly; she went to the till and counted the money out on the counter.

I thanked her and went out.

Outside I lit a cigarette, anxious lest a schoolmaster might catch me.

No, it couldn't go on like that. I had to get away otherwise I would suffocate.

Heinz was going to tell his father that we both wanted to go to sea and I was going to tell my mother. Perhaps it would be best to do so without more delay.

At home I gulped my supper and went to my small and narrow room overlooking the courtyard, with its camp bed, table, chair, washstand and small bookcase. From close to the window you could see a small bit of the sky.

Above my bed was a picture of Vasco da Gama, my favourite of all the great seafarers of the past. I read the story of his life again and again; how as a man of twenty-seven he started off with three ships hardly bigger than fishing smacks; how he sailed around Africa suffering incredible hardships; how he conquered India and then returned, greeted by the King and acclaimed by his people.

If only I could get away to a life of adventure like that. But my mother had no money; that was the obstacle. I had ninety-one Swedish crowns which I had earned as a guide at the Leipzig international trade fair. Would ninety-one crowns be enough for the Seamans' College?

Perhaps! And if not, then I could go to sea without training. That was my last thought on going to sleep.

Next morning Heinz Frenkel came to fetch me on his way to school.

'Well, I had a talk with the old man,' he said, 'and he was surprisingly sensible for his age. He said I was to do my school-leaving certificate first and then if I still wanted to go to sea he would put nothing in my way.'

'Well! well!' I said.

'And you?' asked Heinz. 'What did your old lady have to say?'

'Well, nothing, because I haven't spoken to her yet.'

Laughing, he slapped my shoulder. 'Well, then, old boy we shall just have to go on getting corns on our bottoms.'

I did not feel like laughing. That afternoon I went by myself to the Vocational Council at the Labour Exchange, to enquire into the prospects and the training of a cabin boy.

Certainly no Portuguese king received me. A pale yellow face gazed at me in disapproval behind thick spectacles and said: 'So you want to join the Merchant Navy, a twerp like you? What do your parents say to that?'

'My mother has agreed,' I lied.

He said incredulously, 'Then you had better come back with her,' and returned to his papers as if I were no longer there.

I took heart and told him that first of all I wanted to find out what I had to do about joining and how much it would cost and so on.

He looked up, annoyed, pulled a paper out of the rack behind him and threw it on the table in front of me without wasting a word. It was a prospectus of the German Seaman's College at Finkenwarder.

I thanked him and went.

Outside I inspected the pamphlet. I didn't look at the pictures; I barely glanced at the text; I simply looked to see how long the training lasted and how much it cost There it was: three months' training and a sum of paper marks which made me giddy. Moreover the fees were subject to increases without notice.

I went along the street. At the office of the *Leipziger Neuesten Nachrichten* I studied the financial page and began to calculate.

What luck! My ninety-one Swedish crowns were just enough.

I ran home.

My mother sat in front of her easel painting. It was a forest scene with a few deer in it. I knew it well for she had painted it many times already.

'Just fancy, my dear,' she said, 'the dentist will take a picture in payment. He likes my pictures and he has already found me two new customers.'

Her cheeks were glowing.

'I can ask at least thirty gold marks for each he told me. If things go well I can paint two or three a week. That is 240 to 300 marks a month, my boy. Do you know what? We can stop this rubbishy trade in lace now.'

I looked at her. She was again in the cloud cuckoo land of her dreams. I took a deep breath.

'That's fine, mother, but look here, wouldn't it be easier for you if you had one hungry tummy less to cope with?'

She lowered her palette, 'What do you mean, Günther?'

'I thought it was about time I started thinking about earning some money.'

'And what do you propose to do?'

'I want to go to sea.'

She got up; we gazed at each other.

'Look,' I said quickly, 'I got a syllabus of the Seaman's School in Finkenwarder. The fees are quite cheap and I can pay them myself out of my Swedish money. And then…'

She interrupted me. 'Do you really want to go to sea?'

'Yes,' I said, 'I really want to go. You know that, don't you?'

She said nothing. She lowered her head and then in a small unsteady voice: 'Well, if it's like that I can't stand in your way.'

Two
Under Full Sail

The Seaman's College in Finkenwarder was a large red brick house close to the river. During the day we could see ships sailing past and at night lights would move along the river. When we lay in the dormitories and couldn't see anything we could still hear the sirens of the steamers and we longed to be aboard them, sailing into the unknown.

We were a crowd of thirty to forty young boys, as hungry as wolves, always cheerful and always full of hope.

Discipline in the school was strict. Anyone caught smoking was made to eat the cigarette. But we didn't care. We took what we could from life, even if it were the principal's dinner. It required a special technique to pinch Captain Oelkers' food, a trick which was passed on from one generation to another.

When the dumb waiter passed our mess-room you had to swap the full dishes for empty ones. If you were clumsy you could be badly caught in the lift. But it was done again and again and sympathetic souls maintained that the reason Captain Oelkers was so small was because he often found nothing but air on his plate.

Besides that, we also learnt knots and splices, the signalling book and other mysteries of seamanship. It was all very rapid because we had to be done to a turn in three months. Old salts used to call our school the 'matelot sausage machine' of Finkenwarder.

All the same we were impatient and on our free afternoons spoke of hardly anything but our chances; the chance of being taken on for a long voyage. So we walked with a sailor's roll, up and down the harbour, like old salts, spat over the pier into the water and waited eagerly for someone to sign us on. But no one ever did.

At the end of three months there was an examination. All passed and Captain Oelkers shook each of us by the hand wishing us all a good voyage through life. Then the others went and only two of us remained. Jahnke and me. We hadn't the money to return home and moreover we didn't want to let any chance slip by. So we became 'D' scholars, the leftovers. You began with 'A' at Finkenwarder. You became a 'C' in the month of the examination. 'D' scholars were those mouldy birds who were fed until they too managed to find a berth.

It was not a pleasant time. Our casual mooching along the harbour had turned into a feverish race from ship to ship. But nobody would have us. One evening as we returned to school tired and discouraged Bo'sun Schmidt stopped us in the large hall and said, 'They say at home that after two days a guest and a dead fish begin to stink.' He tipped his ship's cap at us and went.

No. It was really not a pleasant time. When one morning Captain Oelkers ordered us to report to him we were relieved. This would be the end – one way or the other.

As we entered his room we found him behind his desk. We saluted and stood to attention in front of him.

'The full rigged *Hamburg* is looking for two boys,' he said in a sharp tone of command. 'She is a good ship and her skipper is one of the best seamen I know. You can sign on tomorrow.'

'Very good, sir,' I said.

But Jahnke said drily, 'And what wages do we get?'

Captain Oelkers frowned.

'Wages?' he repeated, with disapproval. 'What do you mean? You are still learning and you're nothing but a nuisance on board. Anyhow, the *Hamburg* is a training ship. The Company demand thirty marks a month for the training. And that is cheap, boys, damned cheap.'

I saw Jahnke grow red. He was the son of a peasant in Pomerania and the business instinct was in his blood. 'We can't possibly manage that, Captain, and anyhow my father wouldn't pay it.'

'All right,' said Oelkers, 'what about you, Prien?'

'I don't think my mother can pay it,' I answered.

'Very well, I'll think the matter over.' We were dismissed with a disdainful wave of the hand. In the evening the captain called us again.

'Look,' he said gruffly, 'I have fixed it so that you don't have to pay anything.'

'And our wages?' asked Jahnke again.

Oelkers looked at him for a long time. It was a curious look, half startled and half annoyed, and yet there was also grudging appreciation in it. Then he said, 'Rising in small increments from zero marks,' turned on his heel and left us standing there.

Next day we went on board. It was Sunday, a cold clear day. The sun was shining on the snow and in the Elbe glittering ice flows were drifting down stream. The *Hamburg* lay moored to the pier just opposite Blohm & Voss. They must still have been loading her, for all over the deck lay rope ends and miscellaneous gear, and in a corner we saw a heap of empty tins and ashes.

Nobody seemed to be on board. By the rope ladder stood two men, an officer in a blue coat and a huge man in civvies. He looked like a walrus with red cheeks and a drooping moustache. His shirt was open in spite of the cold and a mighty red throat seemed to grow out of it. Like a garland a thick golden watch chain was stretched across his waistcoat.

'Are you the two new Moseses?' asked the walrus in a deep bass voice as a pennon of gin fumes wafted out of his mouth.

'Yes, sir, we are the cabin boys,' I answered.

'Ah, the gentlemen from the Seaman's School,' he said, and glanced quizzically at the officer. Then he bellowed across the deck, 'Stocks!'

After a while a sailor appeared.

'The Moseses!' said the bo'sun. 'Show 'em lockers and bunks. That one' – he pointed with a thumb to Jahnke – 'goes to the fo'c'sle, and take tich aft to the Jews' temple.'

He turned round and spat into the water. Stocks sent Jahnke forrard where the ordinary seamen and the ship's boys bunked down and he took me aft. I looked at him sideways.

He was a small thin man with a pale and discontented face. His front teeth jutted out and in profile he looked like a disgruntled rat.

The Jews' temple was the quarters for the old lads. It lay close behind the main lift. It was large and low. Right and left on the wall were the bunks in two tiers; dark caverns they were. In the centre stood a long wooden table and two benches. The sun came in through the portholes and was reflected in the panelling and cut long shafts of light through the gloom. There was a smell of seaweed, tar and sea water. Nobody was visible but we could hear someone turn in the darkness of the bunks as we entered.

'That's your bunk,' said Stocks and pointed towards the cavity right aft.

I threw my sea bag into it. Stocks sat down at the table, pulled out a newspaper and began to read.

'You were supposed to show me my locker,' I said.

He lifted his head.

'Wassat?'

'I wanted to ask you to show me my locker.'

He got up and came towards me. He walked without noise, his head pushed forward.

'Wassat?' he repeated. He gave a queer emphasis to the sound.

'I wanted to ask you…'

The next moment I had his hand in my face. Once, then again and again, he hit with the back of his hand.

'I'll teach you to be familiar with a matelot, you blockhead,' he screamed.

I was so astonished that I didn't try to parry the blows.

Then I saw red. Right! Let the bastard be ten years older than me, let him be stronger and tougher, I wasn't going to let myself be beaten like that! I pulled in my head and clenched my fist

From behind a hand laid hold of my shoulder and held me as in a vice.

'Steady boy, steady,' said a sonorous voice, and then to Stocks, 'off, you twerp.'

I turned. It was the sailor in the upper bunk. I couldn't see much of him, only his arm which was still on my shoulder. A mighty arm, thick and hairy and with muscles like ropes.

Stocks trotted to the door babbling so that one couldn't understand the words; then the door banged shut.

The man swung his legs over the edge of the bunk and came down.

'I suppose you are the new Moses?' he asked.

'Yes.'

'What's your name?'

'Günther Prien.'

'And I am Max Witaschek,' he said, and gave me his hand. He was a good two feet taller than I and nearly twice as broad.

'You must not worry about this,' he said, 'Stocks is a stinker. Because he is a weakling himself he looks for weaker ones and tries to take the mickey out of them.'

'I am not weaker,' I said, 'that hasn't been settled yet.'

'Yes, it has,' he said and laughed at me. His eyes were bright as if washed by wind and salt water.

'Yes it has,' he repeated. 'You would certainly be the weaker one because if you'd really got Stocks down we should all have beaten you up: that has to be the way for the sake of discipline.' He sat down heavily at the table and began to fill his pipe.

'I saw that done, once,' he said. 'There was a Moses who hit back; he was a strong lad and he gave the matelot what for. But afterwards he lay for three weeks in his bunk and had to get a new set of aluminium teeth. He used to polish them with emery cloth. I should have been sorry if I'd had to help Stocks,' he added as he lit his pipe.

While he was sitting at the table puffing quietly I stowed away my gear. I hadn't finished when Stocks came back and told me to go aft to the bo'sun.

The bo'sun lived alone in a cabin; he lay on his bunk, his booted feet resting on a stool.

'What ho! Mr Moses,' he said. 'We've been waiting for you, because I've got a very important bit of work for you.' He rolled out of his bunk, stomped in front of me over the deck towards the door under the fo'c'sle. He flung the door open.

'That's our parliament,' he said pointing to two latrine seats. 'You wouldn't believe it: they were white once. Now get on with it. Get hot water and salt from the cook. When you've finished report back to me.'

He went, and I began. Through the open door I could see a bit of the deck and the main mast that rose slender and tall into the pale blue February sky.

So that was the sea life I had been dreaming about. Damn it, it was not a very happy beginning to my life at

When I had finished I reported to the bo'sun. He said nothing but went forrard with me. He inspected the two seats with searching care.

Then he turned, 'Well done, Moses,' he said. His tone was hearty and free from sarcasm. 'If you carry on like this you will always have a good friend in Harry Stoewer.'

He gave me a pat on the back of the head and went.

In the Jews' temple Zippel and I had to look after the mess. Zippel was also a cabinboy, a small quick lad with a mop of fair hair and merry blue eyes. We fetched the tin cans of food from the galley and took them to the mess, where the sailors, seated elbow to elbow at table, shovelled the food down. Roast pork and red cabbage, as it was Sunday.

'You are Günther Prien,' said the other boy when we were seated, 'and I am Otto Zippel, but you can treat me as your equal although I have been on board fourteen days longer than you.'

The sailors laughed; only Stocks looked annoyed. We had that afternoon free. Next day we began work. We took stores on board and I had to hoist the sacks on deck with a hand winch.

Then the sails were bent to their yards. We were standing high in the rigging, turning the sails under and making fast with rope-yard. The icy wind bit our fingers, made the steel yards appallingly cold. The main mast was high as a church tower, one hundred and sixty feet; below us lay the deck, tiny and white. Twenty-eight sails were bent and it took us two whole days.

On the morning of the fourth we were ready. A tug came alongside and at seven o'clock we cast off. It was still almost night on the river and the water drifted past us deep and black. Only the ice floes showed as dimly lit spots in the darkness as they ground against the bow of the ship.

We moved into mid-stream and the crew stood to starboard and gazed across to the land which was still lying in the darkness. Suddenly a hoarse voice cried out: 'Three cheers for *St Pauli,*' and the whole crew yelled as one voice: *'Hoch! Hoch! Hoch!'*

From across the water voices came back which we could not understand. Someone standing next to me said: 'Them's the tarts.'

When it got lighter I saw aft by the bulwark a man with a white cap. 'The old man, the Old Sod,' whispered Zippel. The man on the bridge twisted his head to all sides like a cock about to crow and then disappeared into the chart room.

'He's sniffed the wind,' said Zippel, 'and now he is going to set the course. He can smell weather three days ahead.'

I glanced at Zippel but his face was perfectly serious. We were towed down the Elbe and reached open sea in the afternoon. There was a light nor'east wind and the sea looked grey green and very cold. Towards evening, shortly before sunset, the tug cast off and steamed back.

Now came the command to set sail. We climbed up to the yards. One sail after the other unfurled and bellied in the wind. The sun went under a cloud bank and in the east the moon slowly rose, round and full until shafts of light glittered across the sea.

We laboured until our shirts clung to our bodies in spite of the cold. From time to time I noticed the play of moon-light on the white canvas.

When I stood on deck again a beautiful sight greeted me: Three silvery towers rose before me, their points vanishing in the night sky. The wind sang through them, and from below came the deep and even swish of the breaking bow wave.

We were sailing.

It was as though an invisible power had taken hold of the ship and was pulling it along gently but irresistibly with no noise of machinery but only that deep and even sound.

We had good weather up to the Bay of Biscay, where the wind changed and we had to tack for a time. But we counted on making up for the lost time beyond the Azores, when we would get into the trade winds.

When we got to the Azores there was no trade wind, only light irregular gusts like the coughing of an old man.

Although the Captain ordered every rag of canvas to be set we never logged more than ten miles sea a day.

It was as if the sea had turned to liquid lead. The days were sultry and the nights worse. We couldn't stick it below decks and when we were watch below we lay on the hatch covers to catch the cool night air. The Captain was rarely seen. Most of the time he lay in his deckchair behind the wheelhouse. Occasionally he would appear about midday in the full heat of the sun, a long thin ghost in a pink silk shirt. He would gaze anxiously at the flapping sails and disappear shaking his head behind the wheelhouse again.

Although we saw little of him, he was in the background pulling the strings. We called him the Old Sod.

One midday, Kramer, the donkey man, sent Zippel to the galley for tinned milk. He wanted to sweeten his noodles; but Zippel came back without the milk.

'What the hell do you mean?' Kramer asked rudely. He was a clumsy East Prussian who rarely opened his mouth.

Now he was in a rage. 'Won't that damn hash-slinger give any'.

'No,' said Zippel, anxiously. 'He would, but the Old Sod has put the block on; says we've got to economise.'

Kramer and the others at the table said nothing. Stocks' voice broke the silence: 'There will be something special tomorrow: salt meat and dried potatoes.'

That had been our daily diet for three weeks: Stocks' satire was more than funny.

There were no further consequences; from that time onwards there was no more milk, morning, noon or evening.

Three days later – I was mess boy again – I went to the galley to fetch the gun-fire. Gun-fire was the coffee dished out at four o'clock in the morning. It was black and hot, tasted strongly of chicory and faintly of coffee, beloved of all seafarers from the arctics to the tropics.

'No more gun-fire!' said the cook with sarcasm.

'And what am I to tell 'em aft?'

He shrugged his shoulders, 'You can tell 'em what you like; the Old Sod's put the block on.'

Sailors are not quick-witted. When I returned to the Jews' temple rattling the empty can, my message silenced everyone as before. They sat in their net shirts or naked from the waist up; in front of them on the table lay the hard tack they were going to eat with their coffee.

I don't know who started it. I think it was Moeller. He took his biscuit, drummed it on the table and began to sing: 'Travel…travel…travel…'

This was the alarm call used to drum the watch below out of their bunks in the morning; the joke was no longer a new one. For with the drumming the weevils left their quarters in the cracks of the biscuits and ran along the table. Then they would be swept on to the floor and squashed under foot. It was an old joke. But this time it was more than that. The crew grasped their biscuits and drummed on the table as their hoarse voices rose in dissonant chorus: 'Travel… travel… travel …'

In the midst of the noise the voice of the Old Sod was heard. He had descended the companion way from the bridge and was standing directly above us on the flat roof of the Jews' temple.

'Bo'sun,' he said, 'I think you should see that there is silence in the after-quarters.'

The raucous voice of the bo'sun boomed out: 'Damn your eyes! Silence in the Jews' temple!'

'A nice man,' said a subdued voice, 'he doesn't dirty his voice for us.'

'And so pious and good,' Stocks replied, 'as if he had the Lord himself as his bosom pal. You should have seen him on the last voyage in the Firth of Forth. "You won't get under the bridge with your masts at flood tide," said the pilot. "Yes," said the Old Sod, "we'll get under, I've measured it." It cost two quid for the pilot to wait for the next ebb tide and he wasn't going to waste that money.

"OK Capt'n, but it's your responsibility," said the pilot, but the Old Sod said nothing and went into the chart-house.

I was hammering rust on the fore-mast and Iweisen, the second quarter-master came along and said: "Hey, Stocks, just take a squint into the chart-house, you'll see something worth seeing."

I went and looked through the window; the Old Sod had folded his hands on the card table and was praying to the Good Lord to let him keep his two quid and his mast-heads and not to punish him for his meanness. There he was down on his knees.

He was at least half an hour like that until we were under the bridge. We walked past the chart-house and had a good look, and by Jesus we got through with whole masts!

But from then on whenever we walked past the Old Sod we always dusted our knees.'

There were few laughs.

'Well, let us hope he isn't going to pray our salt meat off the table,' said Schlegelsperger.

Jessen came running across the deck to the Jews' temple; the door was open and we could see him afar; he came from the galley.

'You mugs,' he burst out, 'Balkenhol is in the galley guzzling milk. I've seen 'im with a large tin at his snout going glug, glug, glug.'

It was as if a valve had been opened to release the pent-up fury. Everyone cursed. 'The swine…the Judas…we'll give it 'im, the son of a bitch…'

Then Witaschek said decisively, like the foreman of a jury, 'We'll beat the bugger up tonight.'

It was a dark night. There were no stars. The sky was blanketed by a low mist, a thin sickle of a new moon occasionally penetrating it.

Our watch below was until midnight. At four bells we crept forrard in our stockinged feet. Balkenhol sat in his galley writing, the door open, and the light of the small oil lamp mirrored on his bald pate. We massed around the fore-mast and Zippel cried: 'Balkenhol!'

He looked up. His prominent dark eyes trying to penetrate the darkness.

'Balkenhol,' Zippel called again: this time there was a beseeching plaint in his voice.

Balkenhol cleared his throat. 'Who's there?'

'Could you give me a bucket of hot water?' asked Zippel.

'No,' said Balkenhol, at once, as always when asked for anything.

For a while no one moved. We began to think that Balkenhol had tumbled to the plot for he was gazing fixedly at us. Then he said, 'Anyhow, if you want something, come in!'

'I can't,' said Zippel. He began to whimper, 'My leg, oh, my bleedin' leg…'

Balkenhol's curiosity was aroused. He stood up, waddled to the door and stepped on deck, peering cautiously around him.

Two shadows streaked out of the darkness and threw themselves upon him. Quick as ghosts the three disappeared under the davits, into the shadow of a lifeboat. Slapping noises were heard just like Sunday's, when Balkenhol was hammering cutlets. Half suffocated, his miserable voice cried, 'What the hell do you want? What's got into you? I haven't done anything.'

'Done nothing?' came a threatening voice. 'You've been cooking shit for us the whole voyage.' A second voice chimed in, 'And you've drunk our bloody milk, you bastard.'

'Me…drunk your milk? Never on your life!'

'Don't bleedin' lie, Jessen saw you.'

Balkenhol's voice rang out. 'That's a bloody lie…I saw the Old Sod's empty tin…there was hardly a drop in it.

But that's just like you; when the Old Sod stops your milk you don't say a word; you kow tow and say: 'Yes sir…Thank you, sir!' and let him kick your arses. Then he takes the piss out of you. Do you think I'd do that? Now you want to beat me up? Why don't you go on the poop and give him a piece of your mind?'

Schonborn, our lookout in the mizzen mast, coughed.

Immediately after, Rudloff, the Third Officer, emerged from the darkness.

'What's going on?' he said in amiable surprise. 'Watch below and not in your bunks?'

'Oh, sir,' replied Kramer pharisaically, 'the night was so beautiful,'

'Yes, it is really beautiful,' said Rudloff and passed on.

He had a lyrical nature and we suspected that he wrote poetry. But by now we had tasted enough of the beauties of the night and crept back into our bunks.

Next morning there was work to be done aloft. I was working on the main t'gall'nt s'l with Zippel standing beside me in the foot rope. Far below us lay the ship. Suddenly he leaned across and asked, 'Are you coming with us? We are going to desert the ship at Pensacola.'

I was startled. 'What do you mean? You want to desert?'

He nodded laughing, 'Certainly, nearly all of us. The whole Jews' temple will be empty and the fo'c'sle too. Then the Old Sod can drum the maggots out of the biscuits by himself.'

The Second Officer whistled and we had to get down on deck to brace the rigging. I was mulling over what Zippel had told me; so they wanted to push off; simply get off the ship at Pensacola. I could easily understand; and honestly I wanted to get away too, the sooner the better. I looked at my hands which were red and chapped and corroded by sea water and I felt the boils on my neck which came from the wretched food, meat as salty as sea water and never any greens.

Push off! That was all very well; but where to?

What could you do in a foreign land without papers or money?

When the watch was relieved we crouched in our quarters and fed. I kept on hoping that someone would talk about it, but they talked little and of other things.

Later on I was free. I went forrard and lay on the cable hatch. It was a sunny day with a deep blue sky. The sails hung flaccid and moved occasionally in the breath of a breeze. They made little splashing noises as if small waves were running against the mole. It made you sleepy to hear them.

After a while Zippel came and sat beside me, 'Well, have you thought it over? Are you coming?'

'What are you going to do when you get there?' I asked him.

'You'll see,' he said grandly.

'So you don't know?'

He puffed once or twice at his pipe and looked cautiously around. Then he bent down to me and whispered, 'Man, it's wizard!'

Stocks knows a few farmers over there who are keen to have white overseers. That's the life, you ride across the fields…fifty to a hundred niggers under you sweating and working…and you high up on your horse and just say, 'Come along children, work, work.' At midday, there's turkey and pineapple and every morning, cocoa and the niggers do the messing for you; At night you sleep in a silk bed and the niggers keep guard…'

His pipe was shaking with excitement. I didn't interrupt him. What he said acted on me like the posters of the sunny south we see on railway stations. Only Stocks was the blot on the landscape.

'Who is there besides you and Stocks?' I asked. He counted them out, there were five. The cook was going and Jahnke, who had come aboard with me.

They were not the best of the bunch.

'Is that all?' I asked.

Zippel was annoyed. 'For the moment, yes, but there will probably be a lot more.'

'Mm.'

'And what about you?' he asked and turned to go.

I couldn't come to a decision. 'I guess I'll think it over some more,' I said.

He shrugged his shoulders and sauntered away. He was furious.

I looked up, undecided, to the fore-mast where the sails were flapping in the wind, brilliantly white against the dark blue sky. After all you often heard of people who made good in the Southern States. You might not become a millionaire, but in a few years you could get a little pile together. If I remained a sailor it was obvious that I was going to be poor all my life.

I heaved myself up and went aft to quarters. The Jews' temple was empty, the bulkhead stood wide open. Only Kramer lay asleep in his bunk snoring lustily.

I took writing paper from my locker and sat at the table. Through the open bulkhead beyond the ship's rails I caught sight of the horizon where sky and water merged in silvery mist

I wrote to my mother.

> *Dear Mother,*
> *We shall soon be in America. The voyage has been long and I must say*
> *that I had imagined life aboard ship quite differently. With us it's always*
> *much work and little bread…*

A shadow fell across the paper. Witaschek stood in the opening of the bulkhead. I had not heard him. He had come up silently on his plimsolls.

'What are you doing there?' he asked.

I covered the letter with my hand. He walked up and took the letter away, quite calmly, as if it had to be like that. He sat and began to read.

'Well, well, well. So you are also with 'em. I shouldn't have thought it of you, brother Prien.'

He gazed steadily at me out of his limpid eyes, with a most uncomfortable look.

'What do you mean?' I stuttered.

He waved his hand. 'Don't make excuses, my boy. You know just as well as I what's going on here. But let me tell you something; an honest seaman does not go in for that sort of thing. All right. They've given us sewage to eat on this trip. OK. The old man has been a mean old sod. But to throw everything away for that…the whole voyage…and all that…'

He pointed to the sea, sparkling under the noon sun.

'Can't you feel what it is? Look here, when we get a storm you will see how the old *Hamburg* goes. Then you'll see the old man, boy! Then you won't see a miserable cheese-paring sod on the poop; you'll see a seaman, ready for every kind of weather. But fellows like Stocks can't see that of course; and Balkenhol, with his greasy galley, even less. They just haven't got the vision. But let me tell you something.' He leaned forward and with his fist hammered his words into the table, 'I am not going to see you let yourself in with those burns.'

He jumped up so that the bench fell crashing against the wall. Furiously he stamped out. I watched him, but did not continue my letter.

During the night the wind veered to sou'west and in the morning we could smell land. It was a strange, strong smell, like that of a sun-drenched forest Giant jellyfish floated past the bows.

At two bells the lookout yelled, 'Land ahoy!' An hour later we could see it, a flat white coastline gleaming in the sun. But it was evening, before tacking against the wind, we entered the bay and dropped anchor in the roadstead of Pensacola.

Since our conversation on the cable hatch, Zippel had not spoken to me. On the following morning he approached me again. We stood outside the second officer's cabin door to get an advance of pay for shore leave. 'Well, are you coming with us today?' he asked quietly.

I shook my head. Then we both looked at the land. I was sorry because in spite of everything I liked Zippel. Even if he were going wrong now, he had been a good shipmate.

In Number Two's cabin we came in for a disappointment. ABs got three dollars, ordinary seamen two dollars and the cabin-boys nothing at all.

'An educational measure of the skipper's,' said Number Two, grinning.

After the midday meal we went ashore by motor boat. The town slept in the blinding midday sun. It was a curious town. There were pompous business houses next to mud huts and sheds of corrugated iron and large open spaces scattered with offal and rubbish. On the street the scraggy palm trees were powdered white with dust which covered everything.

I ambled along and looked at the shops. In front of a café brown men in shirt sleeves sweated under the awnings. I could go nowhere for I had no money.

I returned slowly to the harbour. On the long straight road which seemed to lead into the sea, a carriage was coming towards me. It was small, two wheeled, drawn by a mule and loaded with people. I heard them shout from the distance. They were Stocks and company. In the driver's seat, a yellow half-caste with waxed moustache was staring straight ahead. As they passed me they were yelling and waving bottles of moonshine. They did not stop. The cart was too small to hold them all and they hung on it like a swarm of bees. They disappeared in a cloud of white dust.

In the harbour I had to wait for a boat to take me to the *Hamburg*. At last our bo'sun turned up and took me with him.

'Well, Prien,' he said, benevolently, 'had no luck. I suppose the ladies wanted to see your certificate of confirmation?' He laughed and showed the black stumps of his teeth. Aboard I went to quarters. The Jews' temple was empty; everyone had left. The ship was quiet as though asleep and swung gently on the anchor chain with movements of the sea. I crept into my bunk and was asleep. In the middle of the night I was rudely awaken A moist hot breath blew in my face and a hoarse voice murmured, 'Wake up Prien, wake up!'

It was Zippel. He stank of spirits and his face was flushed and cheerful like a child's balloon, clearly visible even in the glimmer of the little oil lamp swinging from the ceiling.

'Prien, we are pushing off now,' he whispered when he saw that I was awake. 'I just wanted to say goodbye and then this lot, here...' He bent down, picked up an iron bound box and let it drop on my feet, 'I couldn't get it into my sea-bag; will you bring it tomorrow to the *Café Chiquita;* tomorrow afternoon about four, yes?'

'But...'

He cut in, 'So long Prien, you're a dirty dog because you won't come with us, but you're my pal, aren't you?' He repeated, 'Prien, you are my friend, aren't you?'

'Shut up!' screamed a furious voice from Witaschek's bunk.

For a moment he stood there staring stupidly and shaking his head like the calf the slaughterer has hit with a mallet. Then he turned and swayed across the step. The bulkhead behind him remained open. I jumped out of my bunk and ran after him. But the darkness had swallowed him up. In the pale light of the stars I could see some figures flitting about, and sea-bags stuffed to bursting point were hanging in the shrouds; the kit of the absconders.

I crept back into my bunk, but it was a long time before I fell asleep again.

As we mustered at the bulwark next morning there were nine absentees: AB Stocks, five ordinary seamen, and two boys as well as the cook, Balkenhol.

The bo'sun who had to detail us for work was in a furious rage. He roared through the quarters and looked in vain into bunks and lockers for the fugitives.

We were detailed for work. With eighteen men instead of twenty-seven it was hard unloading the ballast of refuse which during the voyage had become as hard as stone. We had to break it with picks and then heave it on deck in large iron buckets.

In the middle of this work the bo'sun came to me, 'Prien! The Captain wants you,' he said unctuously rather like a priest at a funeral.

It was the first time that I had been called in to see the Old Sod and my knees turned to water as I made my way aft. In front of the door I took a deep breath and knocked.

He sat at his desk, writing, and did not stop as I entered. I looked around. The room was small but very comfortable; there were leather upholstered benches and the dark brown mahogany walls gleamed like fresh walnuts.

At last he put down his pen and turned towards me.

'You may sit down, my boy,' he said in a friendly tone and I seated myself precariously on the edge of the leather sofa.

A beam of light from the porthole shone on his head; it, was the first time I was close enough to study his face.

It was long and red; his blue eyes lay deep in dark Caverns.

'Tell me, Prien,' he began, 'are you friendly with Otto Zippel?'

He paused and stared at me. I nodded. My heart was beating in my throat.

'And did you know,' he continued in his oily voice, 'that Zippel illegally left ship last night with several others?'

'Yes, sir,' I said timidly.

Suddenly he stood up. He rose in front of me like a tower, poked me in the chest with his bony forefinger and yelled 'Where are they?'

I flinched and had to swallow a few times before I could stammer, 'I don't know, sir.'

Slowly he sat himself down in his chair.

'Oh, Prien, Prien,' he spoke again in the same oily tone as before, 'you *are* in a bad way. You are lying and, you know, you should speak the truth, my son.'

I remained silent.

'I suppose you are thinking in your stupid head,' – he knocked twice against my forehead with his bony knuckle – 'that you are doing your misguided comrades a good turn by saying nothing. But think what fate awaits them ashore: they will be expelled from the Merchant Navy...their seaman's books will reveal the word 'Deserted' and if they start begging in America...and they *will* have to go begging Prien...then they will be chained together by their legs and made to sweep the streets. Think of that, Prien.'

I thought, and imagined Zippel emaciated, a skeleton, in clanking irons, sweeping the streets; but I remained silent.

He talked to me for an hour, and when I left his saloon there wasn't a dry rag upon my body. I had said nothing about the meeting in the *Café Chiquita*.

For dinner there was only cold food as the cook was away. Immediately afterwards I went to the bo'sun and begged for shore leave.

'You're crackers,' was all he said, and that was the end of that.

I went back to the hold and helped the others with the unloading of the ballast

Shortly after three o'clock the First Officer escorted the Captain to the rope ladder. The Old Sod was in a silk suit, white topee and looked severe and dignified.

'He is going to report them to the harbour police,' said Kramer. We stood at the rail and watched them putter away in the motor launch.

'About four o'clock I began to be uneasy. I was thinking Zippel waiting for me in the *Café Chiquita*. Every time we heaved a bucket on deck I looked across the harbour to see if he were on the quay.

At six o'clock we finished work, and were standing at the ship's rail.

'Look over there,' said Kramer, pointing to a rowing boat corning straight towards us from the pier. A coloured boy was rowing and Zippel sat in the stern dressed in white, arms crossed, watching. He appeared to have done himself well, and was showing off.

A second boat shot out of the harbour, a motor launch, also corning towards us very quickly. To the right and the left of her was a huge moustache of white foam, in the stern of the launch stood the tall figure of the Old Sod.

The distance between the two boats diminished. Zippel watching his boy rowing noticed nothing.

In the meantime the whole crew of the *Hamburg* had collected at the rail and was watching the spectacle. We stood there spellbound. Only Witaschek showed courage: he waved to Zippel and pointed to his pursuer.

Zippel, blinded by pride, did not look back. When he came within hailing distance he put his hands to his mouth and yelled to us, 'I'm a free citizen of the United States!'

The Old Sod was now close behind. Startled by the noise of the motor, Zippel turned, and in the next moment was wriggling like a white rabbit at the end of the arm of a hunter.

The launch made fast at the rope ladder. The Old Sod, his hand on the scruff of Zippel's neck, moved rapidly to the Captain's cabin, aft on the bridge.

I did not see Zippel that evening. He returned to quarters after I had gone to sleep. Celebrations in honour of his return had taken too long. Everyone had wanted to greet him. First, second, and third mates, and last and enthusiastically, the bo'sun.

The next day, Sunday service was set for ten o'clock. The service was always kept on land, but at sea only if the weather was calm. Everybody had to be present, even the agnostics; the Captain insisted on that.

'He is a man from Eastern Frisia,' said Kramer sarcastically. 'Since the time they ate Saint Boniface they got holiness in their bellies.'

First we sang a song. The Old Sod took his violin out of its case and blew the dust away. He deliberately rubbed his bow on the colophonium and said unctuously, 'We will now sing hymn number sixty-seven.' He put his fiddle under his chin and intoned with a high and scratchy voice.

> *The Lord has brought us thus far*
> *By His bounty great and kind...*

Zippel stood beside me and sang. He praised God with a crooked mouth because his face was swollen after the bo'sun's greeting.

Three
Shipwreck

We sailed from Pensacola on the third of September. Not counting the super cargo there were twenty hands aboard. None of the other deserters had returned. It was early morning, the sun still below the horizon. We weighed anchor and sang the shanty of the *Return Home*. I think this is the most beautiful shanty there is; it is sung only once on every voyage when the ship weighs anchor for the last run home. The bo'sun sang first, and then the others joined in, in rhythm with the capstan:

> *Rolling home, rolling home,*
> *Rolling home across the seas,*
> *Rolling home to my old Hamburg,*
> *Rolling home, my Land, to thee.*

Then the sails were spread and a few hours later Pensacola lay far behind, pale, distant and unreal, as though we had never walked its dusty streets.

We were on the high seas again. One morning the ship's bell rang. Once… then again…then faster and faster – and louder and louder until it sounded like the bell of a fire engine.

Luhrmann and I were standing aloft in the foot ropes bending the t'gall'nt s'l.

'Fire in the ship,' he yelled, sprang to the shrouds and descended with the deliberate swiftness of a spider closing in on the fly caught in its web.

I climbed hastily after him. I tried to see if I could spot where it was burning. Nothing was to be seen save the white sheets of canvas, filled by the wind.

The deck was deserted; all the crew were standing on the fo'c'sle, the Old Sod, the First Mate, and all hands of the free watch. A cloud of black smoke belched out of the cable hatch and dispersed in the rigging of the foremast

We ran up. The heavy biting fumes robbed one's lungs of breath.

'Damn it, the cable hatch is alight,' said Luhrmann softly.

The Old Sod turned round and gave him a severe look. We stood still gazing at the belching smoke. Harry Stoewer and two sailors were holding a rope above it.

Then a hoarse voice called out of the smoke: 'Haul away!' They pulled slowly and evenly. Slowly, the head of a man appeared, then his chest, and finally his body. It was Witaschek. They carried him to windward and laid him on deck. Teyson followed out of the cable hatch, smoke blackened, with streaming eyes and shaking with fits of coughing.

I dashed across to Witaschek. He was lying on his back, eyes closed, and looking like a dead man. The Old Sod hastened up to Teyson: 'What's it like below? Is it a big fire'

'I think so, sir,' coughed Teyson, 'the rope ends are smouldering like tinder.'

The Old Man turned to the First Officer: 'Take a look in the hold, mister. I think we should move the sacks of wheat away from the collision bulkhead.'

His voice was as oily as ever; only his S's hissed louder than usual.

At that moment Witaschek sat up. Someone had emptied a bucket of water over his head. He looked about him, dazed, then said in a toneless voice, 'The petrol cans,' and then again louder, 'The petrol cans!'

We knew what he meant and the thought was a chilling one. There were six large containers of petrol in the cable hatch. They could explode and set the ship ablaze.

'Give me a line, I'll fetch them,' said Teyson. No one had taken much notice of this tough, sinewy man before. After Balkenhol's departure he had taken over the galley as no one else would take it on. 'I'll get the cans,' he repeated with determination and tied the line round his waist

Someone tied a wet handkerchief in front of his mouth and nose. He disappeared into the darkness of the cable hatch, a fire extinguisher under his arm. We heard him call; the First Mate and the bo'sun reached down and lifted one can after another out of the hold. We were ordered to man the pump but found it broken. The sailmaker was hastily put to work sewing buckets of sailcloths for us to draw up water.

As we returned forrard they were hauling Teyson out. He was groaning and his face was black. His clothes were singed and smoke was coming from them. They tried to question him but he waved them aside and swayed over to leeward, where he grasped the rail and vomited. Then he sank to his knees. Number Two was by him in a flash 'What's the matter, Teyson?'

He made a few snapping movements with his mouth like a fish out of water, but no sound came; then he pointed to his leg.

Number Two pulled his knife and slit Teyson's trouser leg open. The leg was an angry red and blistered and under the knee the skin had burst and was covered with a black crust

'Third degree burn,' Number Two murmured to himself. He turned and yelled at us. 'Don't stand around scratching your arses! Come and get hold of him and bring him aft.'

The Old Sod stepped up, 'Was the fire extinguisher any good?'

Teyson shook his head, 'It's burning too much,' he said weakly.

The Old Sod shouted at us to put out the fire. His voice resounded like a trumpet across the deck.

Work began.

It was terrible. For thirty-six hours we dragged water in buckets and tipped them into the large funnel of sailcloth which the sailmaker had rigged over the cable hatch, dragged empty buckets to the shipside, filled them, and poured them down the funnel.

There was no watch below. All hands were on deck. At times we climbed the shrouds to furl the sails, for the wind was freshening.

Breakers swept over the deck and drenched us to the skin. Our wet clothes stuck to our bodies. There was no time to change.

We filled the cable hatch with water; then the galley bunker; then the chain locker, for the fire had attacked the partition walls.

Late in the evening of the second day, the fire was out.

We collapsed like empty sacks where we stood. We dropped asleep on the deck, on the hatch covers, wherever we fell. The whole ship slept. Only two remained awake, the lookout and the quartermaster.

A boot in my side woke me. 'Boy, wake up. You're not dead.' I glared at the bo'sun, dazed with sleep. 'The First Mate wants you aft, Prien.' I staggered up and made my unsteady way aft.

Number One was sitting under the oil lamp in his cabin reading.

'Can you cook, Prien?' he asked.

I knew at once what he wanted.

'A little,' I hesitated, 'only a very little.'

'Well, I guess it will be good enough for the galley till Teyson is fit again.'

I grimaced. He who wants to be a sailor finds no fun in being a cook.

'You'll get ordinary seaman's pay,' tempted Number One. 'And Zippel can help you as cook's mate.'

So we both moved into the galley of the *Hamburg*. I, with mixed feelings, Zippel overjoyed.

'Man,' he said, 'now we can eat till we foam at the mouth.' Which we did.

But we did not stint the others. Our ambition was to run the finest cuisine there had ever been on the *Hamburg*.

We started our duties on Friday, salt meat day on sailing ships ever since long ago. Balkenhol and Teyson had thrown the pieces into hot water. We knew how teeth and tummy coped with them in our quarters. We put meat and stale bread through the mincer and made rissoles.

After the meal we paraded through the fo'c'sle and Jews' temple and collected our toll of praise. 'Since my last mission cutlet,' said Kramer patting his belly, 'I haven't eaten as well.'

Saturdays it is dried fish day on a sailing ship, but we produced fish cakes and our popularity became embarrassing.

On Sundays it is bully beef with red cabbage followed by roly-poly. There was meat and bread for the pudding; but we couldn't find the cabbage. I sent Zippel aft to the sick bay where Teyson lay groaning in his bunk. Zippel came back: 'There's no more red cabbage; only white!'

I chewed my pipe stem. This would have been our first defeat, for white cabbage was no tack for Sunday.

'Damn and blast it,' said Zippel sorrowfully, 'they'll come and give us a beating up.' He had no illusions over man's gratitude. 'Perhaps we could use raspberry jam,' he suggested.

I shook my head. 'No, there isn't enough. No… wait a minute, wait a minute, I've got it. Run across to the bo'sun and get him to give you some red lead. And if he asks you what you want it for tell him we want to paint the galley.'

Zippel's face cleared up and whistling through his teeth he rapidly disappeared aft. When he carne back we first made a colour test in an old tin. No red cabbage could have been redder.

Its taste was approved. At dinner the orderlies had to come back three times for cabbage. We did not take part in the general feed but ate such of the stores as our fancy dictated us. There was asparagus, cocoa and roly-poly for the galley hands.

It was a wonderful day, clear and calm, and there was certainly no reason why anyone should want to be seasick. But four hours after dinner AB Schlegelsperger went over to leeward, leaned over the rail and let his dinner drop out of his mouth like a landlubber in wind force number six.

Half an hour later every thunderstool forrard in the fo'c'sle was occupied, and in front, impatient men with belts undone hammered with both fists against the wooden doors. On the bridge the Old Sod stalked up and down with a greenish face. From time to time he disappeared into his little hut where a gilt-edged bowl was ready for his sole use. Another half hour and there they were, crouched side by side in the big net under the bowsprit dropping manure onto the meadows of weed on the bottom of the sea.

'Shitting on the piss,' said Zippel and chuckled.

The laughter stuck in his throat; the door opened and there was the Old Sod.

'You seem very happy here in the galley,' he said with a steely look.

I'm sure he spotted the cocoa tin and the asparagus box on the table, but he said nothing. In two steps he reached the stove and bent over the pots and sniffed.

He poked his long finger into the pot of red cabbage, turned like a flash and held a red finger under Zippel's nose.

'What is that?' he hissed.

'Red lead,' said Zippel as if red lead was the proper seasoning for red cabbage.

The Old Sod said nothing. He trembled with rage, like a boiling kettle. I am sure he must have remembered the commandment of neighbourly love; for nothing else could have saved us from the hiding of our lives.

'This is the last straw,' he said, 'you go back to quarters and report for duty tomorrow morning; four o'clock watch.'

That was the dog watch, the worst a seaman knows. We crept away. He called us back.

'I think we had better say nothing about this nonsense to anyone, you understand?' he ordered, and stalked away aft. The Old Sod was a clever man. With opium, castor oil and silence he cleared up the situation in three days.

We made Falmouth on the morning of the nineteenth of October, a sunny, windy autumn day, and anchored far out, as the inner roadstead required harbour dues.

The Old Sod went ashore alone. He returned in the evening and we were told that we were to sail next morning for Cork.

There was depression on board. We had been at sea for weeks, had lain in sight of the coast all day long, had laboured at the anchor chains and yet no one was allowed ashore. During the night the spars creaked in the wind and next morning the old sailmaker, a drip hanging at the tip of his nose, told anyone who cared to listen that he had heard the ship's ghost walking in anger, because of the Old Sod's meanness. We would soon see what lay in store for us.

Up to midday we made good headway, a good ten knots before the wind.

Slowly the wind veered to sou'west as in the south, a pale grey bank of cloud gathered and obscured the sun, all colour became grey.

The wind backed to south; the swell increased and the foam-capped waves quivered with contained force.

I was free at about four o'clock; the new watch emerged in oilskins and seaboots; we retired to our quarters and the warmth of our bunks. The ship creaked and trembled in the fury of the squalls. We could not sleep.

I heard the shrill whistle of the Third Mate and then Stoewer's hoarse command, 'Ready to strike the royals...strike!' Then the sound of tramping feet on deck, of squeaking blocks and rattling chains.

The sailmaker was with us. 'That's just like him,' he said bitterly. 'This wouldn't have happened with Captain Hilgendorf. You should have seen how he rounded the Horn in a storm; he didn't strike a single shred of canvas.'

Nobody answered. We lay in our bunks, tense and curious in expectation of the command, 'All hands on deck.'

'Stupid lot,' said the sailmaker and went out. A gust of wind crashed the door behind him.

Again came the shrill whistle, 'Stand by to strike upper t'gall'nts!' Again the rattling of chains, the squeaking of blocks and the flapping of the slackened sails in the wind.

A report like a cannon shot was followed by a series of whip-like cracks. I stuck my head through the porthole and saw a leaden sky. The deck was awash with foam and high above me fluttered the tatters of the upper t'gall'nt.

They were striking the mizzen t'gall'nt.

'You watch, when they fetch in the mains'l, the Old Sod will call us out,' said Kramer.

The next moment the well-known footsteps sounded above and the well-known oily voice said: 'I think we ought to get the watch below up, mister.'

We got out of our bunks, furious, even before Stoewer had called, 'All hands on deck.'

Outside guard ropes had been strung and the boats had been lashed fast. The Old Sod was standing on the bridge, a narrow silhouette against the dark sky, wearing his white cap.

'It's going to be thick now,' Kramer told me, 'the preacher is going tobogganing.'

'Standby, man clue-garnet and buntlines.'

We ran to our stations, to starboard, and port.

Then we got going.

'Heave! And again, heave!' sang out the bo'sun, and we threw ourselves with all our might into the buntlines till our hands were burning and our bodies soaking. The mains'l fought us like a trapped wild beast. It creaked and screamed and it took over half an hour to secure it.

The bo'sun turned to Witaschek, 'You there, Max! The upper t'gall'nt must be made fast again. Take a couple of boys with you.' He made himself heard above the storm.

Witaschek nodded, 'OK. Come on, Prien and Staabs,' and jumped into the shrouds.

We followed him aloft. The storm seemed to be even greater up there. The mast shuddered under its blows. The shrouds were swaying to and fro and our oilskins were rustling like dried leaves.

At last we reached the sail. Slowly we crept out on to the yardarm. The ship was heeling over to starboard; we were hanging right above the sea ninety feet up, and the bright foam of the breakers gleamed at us from the darkness of the water.

It was almost impossible to control the sail. Again and again the wind blew it out and the wet canvas hit against our legs. It was as if we had caught hold of a goose by the neck and it was hitting out with its wings.

There was a scream. Staabs was hanging from the yardarm his feet waving helplessly in the air. The sails had knocked him from the foot rope. Witaschek sidled along, grabbed him by his collar and heaved him back.

Staabs was ordered to the crosstree and we tackled the sail alone.

It was dark by seven o'clock. It seemed as if the storm had been waiting for the night. With every sea we shipped huge quantities of water on board, which flooded the decks and swept away anything which hadn't been lashed down. The watch stood on the bridge all night for nobody could have survived on deck.

There was no thought of watch below. Again and again the Old Man chased us up into the shrouds. Twice that night we had to tack from starboard to port, set sail and strike again.

The next morning we were eight miles further from Cork than we had been the evening before.

It wasn't the Old Sod's fault. He had done everything a sailor could have done in the circumstances. The storm had been his master.

That day we tacked between Hook Point and Capel Head, but could make no headway. We were wet to the skin and hung in the guard ropes like spiders overcome by an autumn frost

At ten o'clock that evening the Old Sod called the officers together for consultation. They decided to run for shelter to Dublin.

We set foresails and sailed all night and the next morning arrived off Dublin. It was hazy. Low hanging cloud swept grey mares' tails of rain across the sea. Everything disappeared into the mist. The storm held.

Towards eleven o'clock we sighted the long row of spars which mark the harbour road like an avenue of poplars on a foggy morning. We looked for the lightship and buoys but could see nothing.

Suddenly the lookout yelled, 'Buoy one degree to port'; from the bridge came the answering voice of the officer of the watch, 'Hard aport'.

I was standing amidship, a rope in my hand; the Old Sod jumped on to the deck of the Jews' temple and shouted: 'Drop anchor, we're foundering.'

At the same moment there was a dull thud; the ship shuddered. The Old Sod yelled: 'All hands aft, life belts!'

Again there was that dull thud...we were stuck fast on a sandbank. Breakers came over us, sails slapped against each other, the foremast swayed as if it were going to collapse. 'Cut top halyards,' yelled the Old Sod. It seemed as if we were climbing a tree which was being felled.

'Hell,' said Kramer and slowly climbed up the shrouds.

We saw him hanging on the crosstree and drawing his knife; the sails crashed to the deck.

Again there came an ominous thud from below...then another...another...a long rolling rumble...the ship was free. It drifted broadside towards the coast.

A hoarse shout, 'She's steering!'

'To the fore braces; make ready to drop anchor,' shouted the Old Sod.

Slowly the *Hamburg* turned and began to make way. The ship was saved. The Old Sod took a deep breath, which we all heard as he was still holding the megaphone to his mouth; he sounded like a locomotive letting off steam.

Chips came on deck. 'Forrard three feet of water, 'midships three-and-a-half, and aft three-and-a-half,' he reported in a strident voice.

'Is it rising?' asked the Old Sod.

'It seems steady.'

'Right! Check again in ten minutes.'

We moved slowly towards the coast-line, a dark streak in the greyness of the rain.

'Are the anchors ready?' called the Old Sod across the decks. The First Officer signalled: 'All clear.'

Clumsily the ship turned in to the wind. 'Clew up tops'ls, let go anchor,' came the word of command from the Old Sod on the bridge.

With loud slapping noises, the sails beat to and fro. The anchor chain rattled into the sea. A shout from the bows, 'Port anchor chain parted,' was answered by, 'Let go starboard anchor!' and a sudden rattle of chains which ceased as suddenly. Then in the stillness we heard three short metallic blows, as if a steel hammer were striking against the iron skin of the ship.

We stood, frozen, not knowing what had happened. Only the sailmaker spoke: 'The ghost is knocking.'

A door opened. Chips swayed out, took a few unsteady steps and collapsed on deck. Behind him Franz Bohler ran 'Starboard chain broken,' he yelled.

We gathered around Chips; someone knelt down and raised his head; I sponged his forehead; his hair had turned white!

'The chain has broken and the links have cut through the side of the ship,' gasped Bohler. 'Three links went close by Chips's head…bang…bang…bang…all three went into the side.'

'Look,' he cried out, 'his bloody hair has gone white.'

'Clear rockets. Hoist distress signal,' the Old Sod called from the bridge.

A shock went through us. Distress signal! Rockets! This was the end.

The *Hamburg* turned broadside to the storm again and drifted towards the shore. There was no chance of getting any steerage on her; she was drifting helplessly like a block of wood driven by waves and wind.

A crash resounded through the ship and again a crash. We foundered for a second time. The distress signal was hoisted and the rockets were flaring high over the tattered sails of the yards. 'Clear the boats, every man bring his papers,' were the next orders we heard from the bridge.

We ran towards our quarters. Stopping, Jonas grabbed my arm and pointed to the main hatch: 'The rats,' he whispered.

A breaker had smashed the lid of the hatch and there they were, huge fat creatures with pointed snouts and long tails; a true hell's brood.

'Look at the bloody rats,' Jonas repeated.

It was like a signal. Bohler, Jonas and Fleiderer pounced on the animals with yells of rage and chased them over the decks, aiming kicks and blindly hitting out at them with capstan bars. It were as if the pent-up fury of our helplessness and despair of the last few nights and days had found an outlet in a mad and senseless chase. In the end we were all chasing rats like men possessed.

Darkness was falling. It was now nearly five o'clock and with the rising tide more and larger seas were breaking over the ship.

Fleiderer had hit a rat with a capstan spar; he grabbed it by its tail and held it up; the animal was not dead and screamed high and shrill with an all but human voice. It kept on screaming and snapping and trying to escape until Fleiderer threw it overboard.

The Old Sod called down: 'Chips, how much water in the ship?'

After a while the answer came back, 'Forrard four feet and four-and -a-half amidship.'

Shortly after five o'clock, the Kingstown lifeboat came alongside and took us aboard.

The Old Sod sat in the bows, his face as pale as wax. His lips pressed together, he was staring at the wreck of the *Hamburg,* holding the ship's chronometer between his knees.

It was night when we got to Dublin. We were driven through the dark streets of the strange city and lodged in a hostel of the Salvation Army. There was no liquor, only tea and sandwiches. The Salvation Army men sang a hymn in which we were told to join. We didn't know the words but the tune was like one of our shanties. And so we sang with folded hands:

> *Have you seen our old ship?*
> *Ho, Ho, Ho, Ho, Ho.*
> *With its masts all bent like our skipper's legs*
> *Ho, Ho, Ho, Ho, Ho.*

The storm abated by morning and we went over to the *Hamburg.* The deck houses were smashed, there was a foot of water in the quarters. The ship was in a terrible state.

For a day and a night we worked at the pumps. Then the wheat began to swell and we had to drag the sacks on deck and throw them overboard; thirty-four thousand of them, enough to feed a regiment for a year.

We lay fast outside Dublin for six weeks. We were very popular in the town on account of our piety, for the lads of the Salvation Army had praised our fervent singing on the night of the wreck. Moreover we were Germans and a foe of England is a friend of Ireland. They used to clap in the little cinemas whenever German troops appeared on the screen, while the British busbies were greeted with cat-calls and whistles. This, in 1925.

The fate of the *Hamburg* was sealed after six weeks: a total wreck.

The Old Sod flew to Hamburg to report to the owners. We were collected by the *Lützow* and brought to Bremerhaven, as third-class passengers – sailors without a ship.

There we separated. Only Harry Stoewer, Witaschek and I stayed together. We decided to enrol at the seaman's office in Hamburg.

We arrived on a miserable day in December, the day before Christmas Eve. In the seaman's office on *Admiralitats Strasse* a light was burning. The small bald-headed man behind the barrier looked up as we entered and then continued to write. In the background a man in black rose from his chair and came towards us. It was the Old Sod.

'I think we ought to shake hands,' he said holding out his bony hand. We each grasped it and bowed. Then we were given our papers.

Outside Witaschek said quite unmoved, 'He's done it on the cheap again. I would have preferred grog.'

We walked across to the company's office to collect our wages. First they paid Stoewer, then Witaschek. My turn came. 'You owe us five marks seventy,' said the clerk.

'What did you say?'

'I said that you still owe us five marks seventy,' repeated the pen-pusher pleasantly.

He was a brisk young man who wanted to get rid of us quickly.

'But how is that possible?'

'There you are, read it for yourself.' He slid the paper towards me. It was a bill made out to *Cabinboy Günther Prien,* written in the fair hand of the Old Sod himself. It began with a pair of sea-boots at forty-five marks, followed by a long list of cigarettes, cotton, needles and other odds and ends which I had drawn on board.

I stared at the paper.

'Nice prices,' I said.

'With that money you could have bought a shop,' said Witaschek.

He laughed.

But I did not feel like laughing. For I had worked half a year – been hungry – been cold and wretched – and now had blisters on my hands – all for that!

'And how am I to get home?' I asked trembling with rage.

'The company is prepared to advance your fourth-class fare,' said the clerk grandly.

'You bloody…' I began.

Stoewer put his large paw on my shoulder, 'Shut up my boy; take your money and go; you won't get any more out of these bastards.'

I signed and we left.

'Don't worry, Prien,' said Witaschek on the stairs, 'we'll have a quick one now and you can come with us.'

'I'll pay for you,' said Stoewer playing with the money in his trousers pocket.

'And so will I,' added Witaschek.

A sailor with his wages in his pocket is a lord! Stoewer whistled for a taxi and we rode to Pauli, to the women's boxing booths in the *Grosse Freiheit* which Witaschek wanted to see.

The girls were too flabby for him and so we went to *Tattersalls.*

It was only a few steps down the road but Harry Stoewer insisted that the gold-braided porter fetch him a taxi; he refused to take a single step on foot as long as he had money in his pocket.

There was nothing exciting on at *Tattersalls* either, as it was holiday time so we drove to the *Trichter* and from there to the *Alcazar,* drinking at each port of call.

'Very chilly,' said Stoewer imitating the voice of the Old Sod. Finally we ended up on the black sofa at Hermine Hansen's. Witaschek sat on the right, Stoewer on the left and I in the middle.

We drank until the tears ran down our faces and Harry Stoewer mumbled, 'One more trip, Prien, and I'll have all the money I need to buy the *Star of David* in David Street, you know, down by the harbour; it's a gold mine, and I'll be the big noise, and when you come along you'll have free beer and free grog at old Harry Stoewer's till you can't stand any more. Let's drink to it! Hey! Miss!' The sleepy, girl behind the bar swayed up and brought three new grog waters because the rum is left on the table at Hermine Hansen's.

We drank solidly.

After the sixth glass Stoewer blew his bo'sun's whistle and startled everybody in the place. He paid the bill and we left because my train went at four o'clock.

A taxi took us to the station; we rolled up and down the platform arm in arm. The train was already in and brightly lit. We swore that we should never leave each other. The man in the red cap gave the starting signal and I just managed to tumble into the carriage as the train started.

Stoewer and Witaschek stood in a close embrace on the platform and sang:

> *Rolling home, rolling home,*
> *Rolling home across the seas,*
> *Rolling home to my old Hamburg,*
> *Rolling home, my Land, to thee.*

I had weighed anchor for the homeward journey.

Four
Winches and Steam

A few weeks later I was back in Hamburg and I signed on the *Pfalzburg,* a large freighter loaded up and bound for the west coast of South America.

'You've got yourself a nice ship,' said the ferryman who rowed me across. He pointed to an ugly black steamer crowded with derricks. 'When those are working at a hundred degrees in the shade you'll know all about it,' he nodded knowingly.

Then we were alongside. Shouldering my sea-bag I climbed the Jacob's ladder. I was received by a small broad-shouldered man with a round face and flattened nose, the bo'sun of the freighter.

'What do you want'?' he asked.

I showed him my papers. He raised his eyebrows. 'Well, let's have a look,' he said.

'Why not?' I answered. He shrugged his shoulders.

'Run along forrard,' he said, pointing with his thumb to the quarters in the fo'c'sle.

The narrow low room was empty. In the middle stood six bunks of wire netting in pairs, one above the other. There were tin lockers along the walls and two unshaded bulbs gave a chalky white glare day and night.

I looked around me; the linen on the bunks was dirty; the lockers were closed with sea-bag padlocks.

I thought of the Jews' temple in the *Hamburg;* how pleasant it had been there with everything made of wood, the bunks let into the walls, and how nobody had ever locked his locker. There is no such thing as theft on sailing ships.

Hands in pockets, a young urchin, lurched into the room, a cigarette dangling from the corner of his mouth. He stopped and looked at me curiously. 'Where are you from?'

'I've signed on as seaman.'

'Oh, yes!' he said disinterestedly.

'And you?' I asked.

'I am ship's boy here.'

'You don't say.' I thought of my reception in the *Hamburg* when I myself had been a Moses.

'Tell me, are you supposed to talk familiarly with the sailors here?'

Slouched against a bunk, he watched me unpack, and said, 'Sure thing.'

'Well, I won't have it, see? When I was ship's boy I had to be respectful to the sailors.'

He took the cigarette out of his mouth and stared at me in amazement; then he turned round and mooched off. When he was outside he crowed like a cock and ran aft in his clacking clogs.

Half-an-hour later food was called and I went across to the mess, a small room with benches along the walls and a narrow table in the middle. Fourteen elderly men were eating discontentedly, sucking broth through their teeth, the ship's boy among them.

I shouldered myself between two men. As I sat down a huge sailor in shirt sleeves opposite raised his head; 'Ah, the new seaman,' he said, and continued to eat noisily. The ship's boy giggled.

I studied the man. He looked brutal, with a broad face, beetling brows above small, deep set eyes, and teeth like those of a wolf. In the opening of his shirt appeared the tattooed main mast of a full-rigged ship, and on his hairy forearm a tattooed picture of a man and a woman which moved with the play of his thick muscles.

He was Mayland, a beachcomber, the absolute lord of the forrard quarters.

'Where do you come from shit face?' asked my neighbour, a little man with a face like a dried apricot.

'From the full rigger *Hamburg.*'

'I suppose you are working for your bloody ticket?'

Suddenly everyone looked up and stared at me. I realised what the ferryman had been driving at. Clearly a man working for his master's certificate was not popular on board.

'Yes,' I said, 'I am.'

They continued in silence but I now felt a hostile tension in the air. After dinner the beachcomber grabbed my arm as I was leaving. 'Listen, you shit face, we don't stand for bleedin' big 'eads here; we all piss in the same pot here, get it?'

Without waiting for my answer he pushed off, a tower of flesh and bone.

A week later when we began our voyage, we started the deadly routine of a freighter's working day: scrubbing and chipping rust; chipping rust and scrubbing. When we had finished cleaning the stern the bows were dirty again.

The rust was even worse. It appeared everywhere, on the stack, on the bows, on all gear just like mildew on mouldy bread. We loosened it with a hammer and scraped it with a scraper. Then the place was brushed with a wire brush, and painted with varnish, then red lead and finally paint.

This went on from morning to night: scraping, oiling, red lead and paint. You hardly felt like a sailor, but more like a factory hand in a huge steel works floating over the sea.

Whenever I had to stand my trick at the wheel or be lookout I was overjoyed. That at least was a seaman's job.

One day I was kneeling in front of the stack, chipping away paint and thick brown rust, when Mayland's voice sounded behind me:

'Bum sucking, ag'in, eh?'

I did not wish to tangle with this ruffian, so said nothing and continued working.

'So yer won't talk, eh? Well, you'll bloody well listen to me. You can crawl to the bastards on the bridge. I couldn't care less.' He spat at my feet. 'Crawl up their arses if you want to. That's the way to get a bleedin' ticket.'

I felt my blood boil, but held myself in check. I turned and looked at him. He was grinning.

'All right,' I said, 'have your say.' I stood up, hammer in hand.

'You've been to college, and you're a bleedin' big 'ead. That's the difference 'tween you an' me. You get my goat and this is why.' He spat again. 'Number One says to me, "Prien's done better than you. Get a move on. Move quicker." Bloody sauce. I'd like t' see 'im do it. Yap, yap, yap. Prien this, Prien bloody that, yap, yap, yap, yap.' He added to the brown tobacco juice on the deck. I said nothing, and he continued.

'I'm a bleedin' tradesman. They can't soddin' well do without the likes o' me, and I ain't goin' to work me guts out to please them sods up there. Now you know, so keep of my bleedin' way if yer know what's good for yer.'

I was determined to match his crudeness with courtesy.

'Now you can listen to me,' I said. 'It's easy to take advantage and to cheat, and frankly Mayland, if you don't do as much as me, then you must be cheating, because you ought to do more than me. You're older than I am. You're more experienced than I am. And you're getting more money too. Don't blame me if they start riding you.'

He spat again, looked at me stupidly, turned and slouched off, muttering, 'Saucy sod; wants a ticket; I'll give 'im a bloody ticket...'

The voyage was uneventful until we got to Hell, which was the name we gave to the tropical parts of the west coast of South America where the temperature rises 105 degrees in the shade.

We worked day and night unloading and loading, sometimes at four ports in a day. With every hand on board working there were no watches below. I saw very little of the crew because when there was half an hour's rest we dropped like sacks into our bunks and fell asleep without undressing.

One night at San Antonio I was detailed as watch of the hold while others went ashore to drink; I would have been glad to go with them.

The hold was lit by the glaring light of arc lamps; brown mestizo stevedores, sweat gleaming on their backs, were unloading cases of wine from Leixoes. They were nimble rascals and I had to stop them disappearing into the darkness with other goods as well. The hold looked like a warehouse, with piles of piece goods, water closets and pictures of saints, razor blades and carpenters' tools all jumbled together.

During a pause for refreshment at midnight the stevedores squatted below on the quay and I went on deck where it was quiet and cool. The town lay on a rise in the ground sparkling with thousands of lights; it looked like a gleaming wave breaking against the towering Andes behind.

The noise of the returning crew came up from the quay; they were all pretty tight and staggered up the Jacob's ladder to the deck above.

Mayland, the beachcomber, was leading. As he swayed towards me he grunted:

'Watch again, eh? Arse crawlin' again, eh? You snivellin' shit!'

'Shit yourself,' I answered.

For a moment he hesitated, looking a halfwit.

'What did you say?' he grunted.

'The same as you said.'

He took a deep breath; we were facing each other; the others surrounded us in a hostile circle; in the dim light of the deck lamps I could not recognise their faces.

The Third Officer approached from forrard.

The beachcomber turned and staggered off; 'Come aft and I'll knock the shit out of you, if you got the bloody guts,' he taunted, and turned swinging his jacket over his shoulder in a gesture of bravado. The others followed him.

I knew that sooner or later we should have to fight it out. I decided that I would take up his challenge there and then.

As I followed aft I had to force my way through the crowd like a boxer going to the ring. The men were standing in the narrow passage between the mess and quarterdeck, which it appeared had been reserved for spectators and from which you could see clearly into quarters through the open door.

There were only two men in the quarter; Martens, who was lying in his bunk sleeping, and the beachcomber turning up his shirt sleeves and making play with the muscles of his forearm.

I went to my bunk, took off my jacket and hung it on the post

Then we faced each other: one hundred and ninety pounds against one hundred and thirty.

'Give him hell, cock,' screamed Moses; the others kept silent.

I took up a fighting stance, weaving my arms, and danced towards him. He stood like a block; his fists, heavy as sledge hammers, hung slack. He was showing me that he had no fear. 'Come on, come on, you bastard!' he taunted.

I lunged out and gave him a straight right to the chin, but missed the point. Shaking his head two or three times as if clearing his ears of water he came slowly towards me. There was not much room for moving in the space between the bunks and the wall.

He took a wide swing at me; I swayed aside and his fist grazed my ear…a sharp pain and I felt blood run down my neck. Now he came towards me with outstretched hands as if to grapple. I knew that if he once got his arms around me I was done for.

I jumped back. I caught hold of his right thumb and forced it back with all my strength.

He sank to his knees groaning. 'Let go, you stinking bastard.'

I increased my pressure I knew he would kill me if I ever let go. Beads of sweat pearled on his forehead, 'Let go, for Christ's sake let go!' he screamed.

I pressed as hard. as I could; there was a cracking noise…the thumb had broken. 'Christ Almighty!' he screamed then more subdued, in a totally different voice, 'For God's sake, Prien, let go!'

I let go and retreated cautiously a few steps; he remained on the ground holding his broken thumb.

Like many powerfully built men he was not very good at taking punishment.

The others came in and went to their bunks, silently.

I went to the locker and looked into my mirror inside. My ear was nearly torn away by the weight of his blow. I pressed my handkerchief to it and went to the officer of the watch to have it treated.

'And how did you get that?' asked Number Three.

'A box fell on me,' I said.

The beachcomber came in and held out his broken thumb.

I fell down,' he said hoarsely.

Number Three grinned quizzically, 'Well, what d'you know? Prien has a box fall on him and it takes his ear off, and you fall down and smash your thumb. You'd better think up another story by tomorrow morning. If you tell this one to the Old Man you'll get it in the neck, both of you.'

When I returned with my head bandaged a hostile silence greeted me. I pretended to notice nothing and changed. Ten minutes later the beachcomber came back. His white thumb stuck out alike a wax candle. 'The cheeky sod didn't split,' he said, and with that peace reigned once more.

In the next few days we treated each other with exquisite politeness; however fourteen days later at Taltal he left the ship with two others. Wanderlust had got hold of him again, a longing no beachcomber can resist; he wanted to go to Diamantino and he went, although by doing so he lost all his wages.

Although I had peace from then on, I wasn't exceptionally popular because I remained a 'man working for his ticket'. But I had fought the beachcomber and for that at least they respected me.

Five
At The Marine Court

There was a knock at the door, 'Mister Prien, will you go to Mister Bussler on the bridge, please sir,' said the steward outside.

I jumped out of my bunk and went to the washstand. 'I shan't be a second,' I said, turning on the hot water.

Through the window I could see a part of the promenade deck of the *San Francisco* and beyond, the busy harbour of Hamburg. The sun was shining and everything looked bright and pleasing. In the cabin, too, it was pleasant and comfortable, with its large mirror, the cretonne-covered sofa and the broad bunk with many drawers underneath. It promised to be a pleasant life on board this ship.

I put on my brand new uniform, with its narrow gold ring on the sleeve, and adjusted my cap in the mirror.

I was Fourth Officer of the *San Francisco*. With my mate's ticket and wireless operator's certificate in my pocket, the first rungs of the ladder lay below me.

I nodded to myself in the mirror and went out. Number One greeted me on the bridge.

'Will you please go to the American Immigration Officer at the Consulate, Mister Prien, and escort the passengers on board.'

I saluted and left. At ferry number seven I took a taxi.

The immigration office in a wooden shed was as crowded as a railway station, with men, women and children milling around in groups, porters shouting and here and there white-coated doctors edging their way through the throng.

It was the first time I had been in contact with passengers. They pressed around me like blowflies round a sweating horse and plied me with stupid questions. One elderly lady with flashing eyes enquired whether there was dancing on board and if the ship's officers were permitted to dance. A strongly scented man desired to know whether we had taken adequate precautions against shipwreck.

Finally I stowed the whole lot in a bus and drove to the harbour. On board I handed the chattering mob over to the stewards and went to the bridge to report.

There I found Number Three whom I had not yet met.

We introduced ourselves; his name was Schwarzer.

'Did you get your people on board all right, Mister Prien?' he enquired. 'They're a weird lot. You want to look out for the women; at sea they seem extraordinarily in need of support. I've had some.'

I was rather surprised at this, for with his snub nose and his huge ears Schwarzer did not look particularly seductive.

Just then a small thickset man appeared on the bridge. He was exceedingly elegant in a dark overcoat, bowler hat and grey spats. Schwarzer stood to attention. It was the Captain. I introduced myself and made my report. There was a short searching look out of small grey eyes, a murmured, 'Thank you, Mister Prien,' and he disappeared into his cabin.

'He'll put us through it all right, you'll see,' said Schwarzer quietly. 'Shooting the stars, keeping the log, checking the baggage, wireless, watch and all that – I tell you, we officers have a dog's life.'

We were walking up and down the bridge side by side. Wrapped in thick coats the passengers stood about the deck and looked up at us. Glancing down at them from time to time we felt on top of the world. He was twenty-three and I was twenty-one.

We cleared Hamburg on the eleventh of March. It was a cold grey night and there was snow in the air. It began to snow just as I took over the dog watch at four o'clock and soon it became so thick that I could hardly see my hand before my eyes. We were steaming up the Weser and were about the height of the Hoheweg lighthouse. The *San Francisco* was moving half-speed ahead and the foghorn howled at short intervals.

Bussler was standing on the bridge next to the pilot deciding whether to drop anchor or not, with the blizzard gaining in strength it had to be decided if the ship should anchor. Preparations had to be made in any case.

'Go forrard, Mister Prien, fetch the carpenter and make clear to anchor,' Number One ordered.

I ran down the companion way and hastened to the fo'c'sle. The deck was empty and dark and not a single light was burning. Every now and then the foghorn howled. I hammered with both fists on the door of the quarters and yelled for Chips. After a while he appeared holding a torch in his hand, swaying with fatigue.

We crossed to the starboard anchor. Chips switched on his torch and I bent down to look. Suddenly I saw in front of us a huge white light high up right in our course. Turning, I yelled as loud as I could, 'Light right ahead!'

I don't know whether they heard me on the bridge because the foghorn was now sounding incessantly.

The light was rapidly coming nearer. It was barely five hundred yards away, and there was far too little time for me to reach the bridge.

Once more I yelled at the top of my voice, 'Light right ahead.' In front of me moved a black shadow, the lookout man. 'Get to quarters,' I shouted at him. 'Wake everybody and get 'em out.' He disappeared like a flash.

From the bridge came Bussler's voice, 'Hard to starboard,' then shrill and piercing, a steam whistle. But the light remained steadfast right in our course. Through the cowl I could hear the lookout shout, 'Out of your bunks, get out of here if you want to stay alive.'

The next moment an enormous black wall towered in front of me. A violent impact threw me to the deck amidst the thunder of iron crashing against iron.

The ship heeled over to starboard. From the bridge came rapid words of command, 'Both engines stop. Both engines full astern. Hard aport.'

Clumsily the *San Francisco* turned and slid past the high towering sides of the other ship. From above hundreds of gleaming portholes shone down on us. Then like a wraith the other ship vanished into the fog.

I ran below to inspect the damage. One of the quarters was torn open and the cable hatch had stove in. The wind swept howling through the tom steel plates. It was a wonder no one had been injured.

When I came up on the fo'c'sle the starboard anchor was rattling down. I ran across deck to the bridge.

Cabin doors were thrown open and excited passengers emerged. A hysterical woman's voice was yelling, 'Help, Arthur, we're sinking,' and a deep bass voice answered, 'Don't worry, my sweet. I can swim.'

The Captain stood in the chart house. He had just got out of bed and it was clear that he was ill, for his head was burning with fever. 'Didn't you see this ship sooner?' he barked at me.

'No, sir.'

'Did you see what she was called?'

'No, sir.'

He swallowed a curse. The First Officer turned to me.

'Did you see where the damage is?'

'Everything is above the waterline.'

Stepping up to the window the Captain drummed with his fingertips on the panes.

'He really did see something then,' he mumbled.

'Mister Prien, will you try to find out the name of the other vessel,' said Number One. I saluted. The First Officer acknowledged my salute, but the captain ignored me.

Down below in the wireless cabin I bent over the morse keys: *C.Q. – C.Q.* I sent out. *Calling all ships; This is motor ship* San Francisco. *Have just been in collision near Hoheweg. Please give name of other vessel involved.*

No reply came through the earphones at first, but after a while there was a faint buzz.

This is salvage ship Seefalke *leaving Brernerhaven full speed. Do you need assistance?*

No assistance required. I replied.

It would suit these vultures of the sea to give us a tow and then pocket half the value of the ship as salvage.

I waited. At last the calling signal of the Lloyd Steamer *Karlsruhe* came over.

Have collided with you. Please stand by.

There was a long pause, during which I waited apprehensively.

I hoped that nothing serious would happen. The Old Man was certainly furious with me, but I could not think why.

Then again a signal came through:

To San Francisco, *Require no help* – Karlsruhe.

Thank God for that. I jumped up, tore off the earphones and ran outside to report to the Captain.

By now the passengers had all come out of their cabins. They stood about the deck huddled in their furs and overcoats. One of them stopped me, it was the scented one with the dark almond eyes. 'Are you the Fourth Officer?' he asked.

'Yes, sir.'

'Well then, let me tell you something,' he said. 'I heard everything, young man, everything. This is the most incredible and outrageous thing that has ever happened.'

His voice grew louder and more excited.

A crowd of people collected around us.

'You gave orders to awaken the crew,' he turned to the others 'And do you know what he said? He said "get up everyone if you value your lives", that's what he said.'

'Pardon me, I did not say that.'

'What, are you calling me, a liar? Just think ladies and gentlemen, the crew is awakened when the ship is in danger. But we passengers, we can just drown for all they care.' Some of the passengers murmured their disapproval and indignation. The fat man was delighted to have found a public. I learned later that he was an opera singer. 'I must say those are strange orders. I suppose you know, young man, that an officer is supposed to stick it to the last and that it is the duty of the Captain to go down with his ship.'

I should have dearly loved to have given him a slap across his wobbly pudding face. But a passenger is a guest on board and therefore I said, 'If you think you have reason for complaint, sir, will you please speak to the Captain?'

Leaving him standing I went on the bridge.

'Beg to report, sir, name of collision partner, *Karlsruhe*. Fortunately the ship requires no help.' The Captain turned his thick head slowly towards me and said, 'What do you mean, "fortunately"? You are pleased about that, aren't you? If you had kept a lookout this whole mess wouldn't have happened.'

'I do not see where I am to blame, sir.'

He stared at me then turned and went to his door. He addressed me once more, 'The blame will be decided by the Marine Court,' he said, banging the door behind him.

I felt as though someone had hit me on the head with a mallet.

I turned to Number One who was standing by me, 'Do you think that this will come before the Marine Court sir?'

He shrugged his shoulders: 'Possibly.'

'And what happens then?'

'Don't you worry,' he said bitterly, 'the gentlemen of the green table will find a scapegoat all right.

'I nearly had the same thing happen to me in the Gulf of Mexico. One night a raft drifted past us – you know those huge things made out of logs that come down the Mississippi. The thing creaked and groaned and passed. Next morning, they said we had gone past a wreck. The shipwrecked people were supposed to have screamed for help. Five or six passengers reported at the same time that they had actually heard all this. If it hadn't been for a stoker who happened to be spending his free watch below at the rail and who swore afterwards it was actually a raft I should have been in a fine mess.'

My throat became dry. 'Suppose I am found guilty, what would I get?'

'How should I know?' he said impatiently, 'at the worst you will lose your ticket.'

We didn't speak any more but stood side by side gazing ahead into the night that lay black and starless around us. To lose my ticket, that would be the end; all the hard work of those years and then to end up as an officer without papers, even less than an ordinary seaman. The thought haunted me.

At dawn the following morning we weighed anchor and made Bremerhaven at about eight o'clock. At the end of my watch as I crossed the deck to my cabin, I was greeted by hostile looks from some of the passengers. A little girl came up to me and asked gravely, 'Will you go to prison now?'

Experts examined the damage and estimated it at 35,000 marks. After repairs had been effected we continued the voyage.

It was not a pleasant voyage for me.

The Old Man avoided speaking to me. He treated me with a chilly disregard that was more wounding than loud reproaches.

I was surprised therefore when he called me to the bridge one night. We were off San Francisco and the ship was surrounded by fog so that we seemed to be floating through wet cotton wool. The Old Man was in the chart-house. He looked anxious, like a peasant contemplating his dried-up fields.

'Can you take radio bearings?'

'Yes, sir.'

'Then please do so.'

I went on the bridge and took my bearings. The foghorn of the *San Francisco* sounded at short intervals but no answer came out of the white wall in front of us although we were lying on the main steam route of the West Coast When I had taken my bearings I returned to the chart-house and entered my report. The Captain looked over my shoulder.

'That's all rubbish you've got there,' he said shortly. 'This is where we are,' pointing with his finger to a place which lay further to the west

I said nothing.

'Well, Prien, go and get yourself a shore bearing.'

'Very good, sir.' OK I said to myself, if you don't trust me, you can get somebody else to tell you.

In the radio cabin I got the nearest coastal station to give me my position. The new position lay even further to the east than the plotted position.

The Captain waited in the chart-house. When I made my report he stormed. 'Have you completely lost your mind? Anyone with sense can see that this is wrong.' He frowned. 'Your ship's bearing must be wrong; you had better take another.'

I took a fresh bearing.

The new position corresponded exactly with the first bearing I had taken.

The Captain said nothing. He stalked up and down the chart-house, his hands behind his back.

He said, 'I shall go according to the shore bearing.'

'Then we shall be sitting in the mud in two hours' time,' I said.

He stopped. 'If I stay on your course I shall be sailing past the pilot boat and stick in the mud afterwards.'

I knew I had nothing further to lose where he was concerned. 'Sir, I suggest that you first sail according to my bearing; afterwards you can get correction from shore.'

He stared at me like an angry bulldog.

'Very well, but if we stick in the mud then you had better look out; I shall get you degraded by the Marine Court.'

He turned round on his heel and left me. I remained alone in the chart-house. Outside the fog was like a wall and there was still no reply to my signal. I had a very queer feeling in my stomach. If things went wrong then I had had it. I knew for certain that the Old Man would make good his threat.

The sweat was pouring off my body. Half an hour later I reported to the Captain, 'It is time to change course, sir.'

He came in.

'New course forty-two degrees.'

'Very well, go to forty-two degrees,' he said without looking at me. Then he left again.

If my bearings were correct we should now be quite close to the coast and any moment the pilot's boat should be sighted. But there was nothing, only night and fog.

The officer of the watch poked his head in through the door, 'The lookout reports five short bells in front,' he spoke softly in order not to drown the signal. I went out to him on the bridge. We listened carefully, and heard to port, ahead, a weak signal, still some distance away.

Ten paces away stood the Captain, motionless, a dark statue in the fog.

'Sir, pilot boat ahead,' I whispered. My voice trembled a little for this was my most beautiful moment on board the *San Francisco*.

'Do you think I am deaf?' he said. 'I have heard it for quite a time now.'

I returned to the chart-house, the Old Man following me close behind.

'Go down and take on the pilot,' and then as I was already going he added, almost reluctantly, 'well, you did that all right.' This was the highest praise I had ever heard from his mouth.

From then onward he was very much nicer to me. On our return he dismissed me from the bridge when we were still one hundred miles off the coast I was relieved of all duties, and was told to take things easy so that I should be fit should an emergency arise and radio bearings were again required.

But all the time I was apprehensive about the pending enquiry at the Marine Court. True, Bussler thought there would be no enquiry at all, for no one had been killed or injured.

We arrived in Hamburg and I searched through my mail. There was no summons. Nor had the Captain or the First Officer received one.

I breathed more freely. That evening however, Captain Schumacher from the company came aboard. He stayed with the Old Man for a time in his cabin, and when they returned, the Captain said in passing, 'Enquiry at the Marine Court in three days' time, Prien.'

That night I was on watch. That was all right because I wouldn't have been able to sleep anyhow.

At nine o'clock an old skipper came on board, an old man with a bald head and an ice grey beard. We sat together in the empty mess and I ordered some grog and a few ham sandwiches for him.

He told me of his past life, how he had been in command of a ship twice as large as ours for twenty years. And now he was old and past work they had pensioned him of with one hundred and eighty marks a month.

He asked me whether he might take a ham sandwich home with him for his wife and when I said 'yes' he wrapped it up carefully and stowed it away in his pocket with an embarrassed smile on his face.

I turned my head away; so that is what he had come to. But what was going to happen to me?

Three days later the enquiry opened at the Marine Court.

'Now they've got us by the short hairs,' Bussler said.

We were standing in the long dark corridor of the Nautical Court House in Bremerhaven, the Captain, the First Officer and myself, and a few men of the crew. The officers of the *Karlsruhe* arrived a few moments later and there were formal exchanges of civilities.

We were standing in a dark passage in front of the large brown door that led to the courtroom, the men from the *Karlsruhe* collected near a window.

'Well, Prien, they won't have your ticket, anyhow,' said the Old Man, consolingly.

A slim elderly man with a pointed beard and spectacles went past. Everyone saluted. He acknowledged the greeting coolly and disappeared into the courtroom.

'That is the State Commissioner,' explained the Captain. 'He is a sort of prosecutor for the State.'

Behind him came a few jolly red-faced men carrying brief cases. One of them nodded cheerfully at us.

'Those are the Assessors,' said the Captain. 'All people from Bremen.'

'That's not too good for us Hamburgers,' said Bussler thoughtfully.

Finally a small man in a black suit, the Chairman, hurried into the courtroom like a mole into its hole. We were called in by the usher. It was a long sombre hall. Behind the table sat the Chairman with the Assessors. In front of it on the left-hand side was the Commissioner of the State. We stepped up to the table and handed our papers to the clerk.

'I hope we'll see 'em again,' Bussler whispered to me.

We were invited to sit down.

The Chairman opened the proceedings by reading the warrant for the action. Then the Captain of the *Karlsruhe* was called as first witness. He was very sure of himself and declared that the *Karlsruhe* had anchored on account of the weather conditions and engine trouble. He had done all that was necessary; the ship's bell had been rung at short intervals and when we approached he had sounded his siren.

He bowed to the court and returned to his seat. He had made an excellent impression.

Then it was the Old Man's turn. He could say nothing, as at the time of the collision he had been in bed with a high fever.

'In that case,' asked the Commissioner, 'shouldn't you have appointed a second in command to take your place?'

'I didn't know beforehand that I was going to have influenza,' said our Captain gruffly.

He sat down. The first round went to the *Karlsruhe*.

Bussler was called to the witness box.

It would be my turn next, I thought.

They handled him very severely. Why did he not anchor when the weather got worse? He said that it was impossible right in the middle of the sea lane. They asked why he did not go slower. He said he was going half speed.

'Half speed was too fast,' said the Commissioner, 'you should have gone slower.'

Bussler remained silent.

'What did you do then?'

'I sent the Fourth Officer forrard to clear the anchor.'

'Who is the Fourth Officer?'

I stood up.

'So you were together with Mister Bussler on the bridge?' said the Commissioner, punctuating each word with a jab of his pencil on the table.

'Yes, sir.'

'What time was that?'

'Shortly before four o'clock.'

'About how many minutes before?'

That was the trap. I felt it instinctively but I tried in vain to guess what he was driving at.

'About three or four minutes,' I replied, hesitating.

'Ah.' Swiftly he turned towards the pilot.

'But you had said that it was a pitch dark night, the sky completely covered and snowing '

The pilot nodded.

The Commissioner turned to me again. His spectacles were sparkling.

'According to my naval experience I think you would have needed at least seven to eight minutes to accustom your eyes to the darkness. No wonder you couldn't see anything.'

'But I did see.'

One of the Assessors chipped in.

'Your pardon, Mr Commissioner, but when you are young your eyes get used to the darkness quicker.'

I thanked him with my eyes, while the Commissioner made a face as if he had bitten on a peppercorn.

'Very well,' he said grudgingly, 'let us leave that for the moment.'

Then he turned back to Bussler. 'When did you actually first see the *Karlsruhe?*'

'The Fourth Officer reported her to me.'

'Oh, yes and what did you see, Mister Prien?'

'I noticed a white light burning high up.'

'Well, and now tell us how everything happened. You got the order to clear your anchor. What did you do then?'

'I ran forrard and called the carpenter,' I said, carefully considering every word, 'and then we went together to the capstan.'

'So therefore you immediately busied yourself about the anchor?'

'Yes, sir.'

With a triumphant gleam in his eyes he made this point 'And it did not occur to you to look around first I suppose?'

I had nothing to say.

Suddenly the Old Man burst out. 'What are all these stupid questions? The First Officer had the order to clear anchors and therefore the first thing he had to do was to clear them, and that's that. On my ship my men carry out my orders and that's all there is to it!'

His voice had got louder towards the end and the Chairman rang his bell. 'I must ask you, sir…'

All the same I had the feeling that this round was ours. Then Bussler had to give an account of his actions after the collision. He did that very well, detailing them one by one, while the Commissioner tried to shake him with disconcerting questions.

The session came to an end and the court withdrew

We walked up and down the old corridor outside.

'How do you think it's going, sir?' I asked the Captain.

'It's a toss-up.'

At last we were called back into the courtroom. 'The court filed in and the Judge rolled out the judgment of Court.

It was only the weather that was responsible. Every else was blameless.

It was as if a weight had been lifted from my chest we walked down the stairs together, Bussler asked me what I was going to do now. I said firmly, 'Now I am going school for my captain's ticket.'

Six
Out Of Work

Towards the end of January 1932 I passed my captain's examination. I had thought that it would see me over the stile and that now everything would go automatically. Instead of that there came unemployment.

After the examining commissioner had shaken me by the hand I had jumped into a taxi and called on everyone, on Hapag, on Slomann, on the tanker company, on Riedemann. It was the same everywhere. A regretful shrug of the shoulders, a sigh. 'It's a bad time,' they all said, and at best the meagre promise, 'we'll take your name in case there is anything, and let you know.'

But I stayed in Hamburg in order not to miss a chance, and lived on my savings. Finally, as nothing came my way I decided to become an author. I bought one hundred sheets of white paper, a second-hand English-German dictionary and started to translate *The China Clippers*, one of the finest books on sailing ships. But when I reached page fifty I ran out of coal and money.

My old shipmate from the *Hamburg* days, Harry Stoewer helped as much as he could. He had taken over the *Star of David* and he said to me, 'You can eat and drink at my place as much as you like. I know Captain Prien will pay me back.'

His trust was touching, but I felt it couldn't go on like that; so one evening I went to the station and took a night train home to my mother.

I arrived in Leipzig in the grey dawn of a February morning. When I walked up the stairs in our house my heart was beating violently; it is not easy for one's pride to come back after eight years, penniless, and without a job.

I rang the hell. My mother opened the door.

'My boy,' she said and drew me into the dark hall. She had greyed in the last few years. Then we went into her workroom. Everywhere, on chairs and the table, were lying models and showpieces for shop windows, sausages and hams made of wood.

I looked at her in astonishment. She smiled.

'I know you used to laugh at my ham paintings but now I am really painting hams.'

She made breakfast. Afterwards I lay down on the sofa and studied the paper, especially the 'situations vacant' column. It was hopeless.

There were hardly any vacancies but on the other hand there were thousands of applications for employment. Gradually I felt that I should be lying there unemployed for days, weeks and possibly for years. I sat up with a jerk. Surely I had friends, school fellows, sons of well-to-do people. Somewhere there must be something that I could do. There must be work, if only I could find it; after all I was hale and hearty and not entirely half-witted. I jumped up.

'So long, mother,' I called into the other room. Then the hunt for a job began, from house to house, and from office to office. It was always the same. Many people had been torn out of their accustomed path, had had to give up their studies and had found a precarious livelihood somewhere to which they clung with grim determination, terrified of losing it and of sinking into the morass of unemployment.

Many, too many, were as badly off as myself. The lounged about, knocked at doors which always remains locked and kept hoping for the miracle, the miracle that was a job.

On the third day of my wanderings I met Hinkelhaus; he had studied law but had not completed his course as his money had given out. But he was not defeated. He had opened a legal advice bureau.

'If you like you can be office manager,' he offered, 'though I can't pay you any wages. We'll go half shares if you care for the job.'

I agreed.

The office was in the *Eisenbahn Strasse*. It was a small bare room with two tables and five stools and a nameplate on the door, *Ernest Hinkelhaus, Legal Adviser* – that was all.

During the next eight days I went regularly every morning, a packet of sandwiches in my pocket, and returned home every night. With the exception of Hinkelhaus I never saw anyone in the office. We discussed the evil times at great length and the ineptitude of the government that allowed huge sections of the population to starve to death. These debates were extremely stimulating, but I saw that if it went on like this my share of the profits at the end of the month would amount to precisely one half of nothing.

Hinkelhaus decided to canvas for clients, and I was to look after the office and the correspondence. I remained alone in the small room, looked out over the grey street, over the roofs to the railway lines, and waited. No clients came. Eight days later The Legal Advice Bureau closed its doors, never to open them again.

I was on the street once more. There was now only one thing open to me, the Assistance Board. So I went to the old building in the *Georgenring*.

Several people were already waiting in the grey and dirty waiting room. They looked completely exhausted, as if privation had emptied them, leaving nothing but a shell. Every time the bell went one of them stood up and disappeared through the door. At last it was my turn. Smoothing my suit I entered. A little man with ashy grey hair sat behind a barrier, writing. He glanced at me over his glasses with a tired bored look.

'Name? Occupation? Date of Birth?'

His pen made scratching noises and his sleeve slid slowly across the paper. 'And why are you reporting after all this time?'

'Because first of all I tried to find work.'

'Well, yes, I suppose so,' he said and handed me a card. 'You will draw your first money in three weeks' time in the *Gellert Strasse*,' he said.

'And what am I to do until then?' I asked.

But he rang the bell for the next applicant.

In the middle of March I went to *Gellert Strasse*. At eight o'clock in the morning a large number of people had already arrived, a long queue advanced slowly in little steps.

Bang, bang, sounded the stamp in front of the office window. The first fellow moved a few steps on…and then bang, another few steps on. This procession of misery moved in a queer rhythm imposed by the thudding of the rubber stamp. It was my turn. I pocketed the few coins and left hastily. The queue had become longer still. The sight of these blunted and hopeless faces, the acrid smell of poverty, the endless thud of the rubber stamp was the most depressing experience I was ever to know. I went out. Now I was downstairs again. Why on earth had I put up with all this? The years on the sailing ships had been no picnic. And now that at last I had got my diploma the ground was cut from under my feet. Finished at twenty-four!

Why? If you asked anyone he shrugged his shoulders and said, 'Well, there's no work, and that's how it is, my dear boy.' Well damn it, what about the people in office the ministers, the leaders of the party, and the officials? Wasn't it their job to see that conditions changed for the better? How could they sleep peacefully as long as there were strong and healthy men, willing to work, eager to work, spoiling like rotten straw?

The miserable few coppers which they threw at us just kept us alive. They gave us the money reluctantly and they feared our despair. They wrapped the money in the page of their newspapers which oozed with beautiful phrase and empty professions of sympathy.

Yes, they could sleep, these gentlemen; they slept very well on the soft cushion of their motto: *Live and Let Live*

But reality had stripped the tinsel from their phrases, we saw life as it really was, and we saw them as they really were. *Live and let Die,* that was the true meaning of our leaders' motto. I was gripped by a fury of resentment against this soft and lying indifference. I joined the National Socialist Party.

Under full sail.

Green water on deck.

Surfaced U-Boat leaves a white wake.

Commander Prien.

HMS Repulse *hit amidships.*

Torpedo inspection.

HMS Royal Oak.

Commander Prien in his conning tower.

The U-Boat…

…and her victim.

Triumphant return from Berlin.

Seven
Labour Corps

I enrolled in the voluntary labour corps. To be on the safe side I wrote to the leaders of several camps. All of them declined my services as I was too old at twenty-four, but Lamprecht, the labour leader of *Vogtsberg,* decided to give me a trial.

'If you care to enrol as an ordinary volunteer,' he wrote, 'you may come.'

Three days later I started for the camp. It was a tedious journey to the *Vogtland.* There was a halt for half an hour at Plauen and I ambled through the little town, with its cobbled streets and its white timbered houses. It was a hot and dusty day towards the end of August and the leaves were already beginning to turn.

I was feeling depressed. Whenever I went to sea I was glad, now I could work up no enthusiasm.

Surely any kind of life was better than sitting around doing nothing? But after all I was wedded to the sea, body and soul, and a seaman on land finds himself in a strange element.

In the garden of a villa I caught sight of a girl, fair and dressed in white. I looked at her and I knew that it was more than a garden fence that divided us.

It was the inspiration of the moment. I put my suitcase down, walked across the street to a flower shop, bought a bunch of roses and walked straight into the garden where the girl was sitting.

The wrought-iron gate squeaked as I opened it. The girl looked up. I walked towards her across the lawn, pressed the flowers into her hand, bent down, and gave her a kiss.

Her mouth opened in speechless astonishment. I stood there for a moment looking down at her and then I turned and left. Outside I picked up my suitcase and walked quickly down the street without once turning round. I went straight to the station.

My train steamed out and in the afternoon I arrived at Olsnitz. The labour camp was situated in a castle which towered above the little town. Previously the grim structure had served as a women's prison. The windows were still barred and, like a honeycomb inside, cell lay next to cell.

An orderly took me to the camp commandant. We passed many doors as we walked along the iron landing which resounded with our footsteps. The orderly knocked at a door and opened it. I stood facing the commandant. Lamprecht, a tall slim man with a hard face, rose as I entered.

'Ah, you are Prien,' he said, 'the young man who wants to start as an ordinary volunteer.'

'Yes, sir.'

He held out his hand. 'Then I greet you as a comrade, Prien. Go to the housemaster and get yourself fitted out. Tell him that you are detailed to *Squad Hundsgrun.*'

Another handshake and I was outside. I received my kit which consisted of a worn-out military uniform, and then I was shown my bunk and my locker. There were seventy of us in the dormitory, a large well-lit hall which had previously been the prisoners' workroom.

I stowed my gear away and waited. The squads were still outside at their labour. They did not return until five o'clock.

I could hear them in the distance; they marched singing into the courtyard of the castle and came roaring up the stairs into the hall. When they saw me they stopped, and a small emaciated fellow advanced towards me and asked, 'Are you the ship's officer?'

'Yes, why?'

'We had heard a long time ago that you were supposed to be coming,' he stammered and retreated behind the others. I looked around me. They were nearly all young fellows of nineteen or twenty, carpet weavers from the large factory down by the station. Most of them looked ailing and worn out; and about all of them was the air of oppression, of men who have lived too long in fear about their daily bread.

They looked at me full of curiosity but no one questioned me further.

On the following morning duty began at half past five. The squads fell in in the courtyard, and received their day's rations of bread, butter, sausage, cheese and a flask of lukewarm black brew which was served up as coffee and which we called 'nigger sweat'.

After breakfast we started out, either in lorries or on foot, according to how far away our place of work was. *Squad Hundsgrun* had to march.

We passed through Olsnitz and then marched along the main road up the Elster valley. The building site we were working on lay close to the village of Hundsgrun, on a long sloping meadow which descended gently to the river. Down below we could hear the murmur of a water mill. Above us a forest extended to the top of the hill.

It was our job to drain the whole meadow. My job was to cut out sods of grass and dig a narrow ditch exactly four and a half feet deep.

From eleven to half past we halted for dinner and sat at the edge of the forest on tree stumps, devoured our food and chatted with each other. Then we continued to work until half past two when we returned to the castle. At half past five we had our dinner which was the only warm meal of the day. After that we were free, unless the camp commandant decided on an hour's drill.

This went on day after day, and after a while I became accustomed to this new life. Only the free evenings and Sundays were boring.

A wide view lay in front of the castle window. The tops of the Downs were thickly wooded and lost themselves in a distant blue haze. It looked as if tall green waves had rolled up from the distance and congealed. I thought of the sea and felt homesick.

One day there was enormous excitement. The camp steward had disappeared. We ran all over the castle shouting and calling but he did not answer. Finally we went from cell to cell. Every time we opened a door a chill and mouldy smell greeted us, for most of them were unused and were as they had been left when the *Castle Vogtsberg* had still been a prison.

At last we found him in a cell in the left wing. He lay on a trestle bed and had a gas tube in his mouth. To make quite certain that he would die he had stuck up his nostrils and the corners of his mouth with plaster. But dying must have been hard for him. His right hand clutched his throat as if at the last moment he had wanted to tear himself away from death. We opened the door and windows, and then carried him out. Then we telephoned for the doctor and in the meantime tried artificial respiration. It was in vain; he was gone. The body was already stiff with the rigour of death.

The vital question was why had he done it? Someone suggested that he had had control of money. But books and cash were checked and found correct.

We examined his locker. There was a bundle of letters from a girl, the last of them three days old. She wrote:

I have been waiting for four years and now I can't wait any longer. You can't get a job and I will be an old woman by the time we can marry…

It was always the same. Want, misery, despair and the future merciless and grey. You had to be tough to stick it.

Immediately after dinner I was told to report to the camp commandant. He was standing on the iron landing in front of the cell. The squad leaders of *Hundsgrun* were facing him.

'Comrade Prien,' said Lamprecht, 'you will take over as leader of the seventh party.'

'What about Reseler?' I asked. He had been leader up to now.

'I am making him steward.'

I clicked my heels and left. I was glad that I was being promoted so soon, although a shadow of grief lay over my pleasure.

At the early morning parade next day my nomination was made official and we went to work again. Life was not much different for me; I still had to cut grass sods and dig ditches.

The year was slipping away and our labours became increasingly hard. October came with fog and rain. We floundered in the mud and more than once we were caught in showers on our way back to the castle so that we arrived drenched to the skin.

We were frequently inspected by the chief of the land commission, a long thin man, a real office corpse. He walked about, criticised everything and played the benefactor, for the labour service was in receipt of a subsidy from the local Treasury.

One morning he arrived in the company of a fat and bald gentleman who turned out to be an inspector from the Saxon Home Office. With the group leader they walked over the meadow, halting now and then by a group and making derogatory remarks. I was certain that they hadn't the slightest idea about drainage, especially the fat one from the Ministry. He would have been quite incapable of lifting a sod of grass.

There had been fine rain all the morning but now it began to pour down in earnest. A thick cloud pushed itself over the edge of the hill and the rain came down on us in sheets.

It was an unwritten law that as long as there was fine rain we had to continue to work, but when it was pouring we could go into the builders' hut at the edge of the forest. The inspector and the man from the Ministry were already there, but we were still working.

We all looked at the leader of the group but he made no move to dismiss us. The men began to grumble and I threw down my spade and walked up to him.

'Say, how long are you going to keep us out in the rain?' He shrugged his shoulders, 'I can't do anything during an inspection.'

'Well, if you haven't got the guts, why don't you fall out and I'll carry on for you?'

'Will you do that?' he asked.

'Of course, certainly.'

'Then I hand over to you,' he said, obviously much relieved.

I waited until he had disappeared into the forest. Then I blew my whistle. The men ran up to the builders' hut and I followed them slowly. The inspector started as soon as I entered. 'What do you mean by dismissing the men?'

'It is raining,' I said.

He took a deep breath; the fat one from the Ministry joined in. 'Where is your group leader?'

'Gone to lay an egg,' I said.

He gazed at me in astonishment; then he said, 'Tell the men to start work at once.'

'I haven't the slightest intention of doing so.'

'I give you a formal order.'

'I get my orders from my camp commandant.'

'We'll see,' said the inspector. 'What's your name?'

'I am Party Leader Prien.'

He pulled out a notebook and wrote down my name.

'All right,' he said, 'and are you now going to order the men back to work?'

'I have already said no.'

'And why not?' asked the fat one.

'I am responsible for the health of my men.'

The inspector said, 'That is enough.' Turning to the fat one, 'Please come along,' he said, 'there is no point in staying here.'

They went out into the rain, and walked down the meadow side by side to the highway, where the car from the Ministry was waiting for them. The little fat one and the tall thin one got in and they drove away.

When we returned from our labour I was called to the camp commandant. The fat one from the Ministry and the thin one sat in

Lamprecht's cell. There they sat in hypocritical solemnity like a couple of schoolboys who, having sneaked to the headmaster, sat back and waited to see the chastisement of the culprit.

'Will you please give me your report on what happened in *Hundsgrun,* Comrade Prien?' said Lamprecht severely.

I gave him a brief account of the events.

'Is that correct, gentlemen?' he enquired. The two nodded.

'As your group leader is leaving us on Monday morning I am appointing you herewith in his place, Comrade Prien. I am in complete agreement with everything you have done.'

'That is infamous,' gasped the official of the Ministry, rising. The Inspector also rose, 'You will regret this, Mister Lamprecht,' he said as he left. Nothing further happened.

Four weeks later, Lamprecht went on leave and nominated me his deputy.

My promotion to group leader had left the camp comparatively unmoved, but I could clearly see by their demeanour that this promotion enraged them. The older people, some of whom had been doing labour duties for more than two years, felt themselves especially slighted. True, they didn't say anything; but when they spoke to me they did so in a strictly formal manner.

I was far too busy to bother much about their feelings.

During the morning I coped with the clerical work; the rest of the day I hurried on a motor bike from building site to building site.

One evening I had a telephone call from the miller who owned the mill in the valley near *Hundsgrun.* A ham had been stolen, and it was probable that one of the men of the squad working there was responsible for the theft.

'When did you discover the theft?'

'Three days ago.'

I promised investigation and hung up. This was damned awkward. If the ham had been pinched three days ago it would in all probability have been eaten by now. At the best the bone could still be discovered. In these circumstances there was no point in holding a parade.

That evening after lights out I ordered them all to file in and organised a search of the lockers. With a torch I went from locker to locker and from bed to bed. The ham came to light under the straw mattress of a boy from Dresden. It was quite untouched, not a single slice had been carved from it.

I ordered the group and squad leaders of the culprit to my room and then I sent for him. He was a small, pale boy with thin protruding ears, the terror of the beaten dog in his black eyes.

'Did you pinch this ham from the mill?'

A long pause, then almost inaudibly, 'Yes, sir.'

'Why?'

Silence.

I stepped close to him, 'Why did you steal?'

He began to cry. He cried silently, only his face puckered up and tears streamed from his eyes. He said nothing.

'Why won't you say anything?'

He tried once or twice but the words were swallowed in sobs and then there was silence. I saw that I could get nothing out of him.

'All right,' I said, 'the ham stays here and you leave camp tomorrow morning. You leave first thing, you understand. You need not attend any further parades.'

He clicked his heels, thumbs against the seams of his trousers. All the time the tears were streaming down his face.

'He is the last person I should have thought would do such a thing,' said the group leader after the boy had left us.

The two leaders went.

I lay down on my bunk, crossed my arms behind my head and considered the case. What a stupid affair, what a nuisance that it should happen during my term of command.

There was a knock at the door.

'Come in.'

Manthey, one of the old hands, stood in the door. In the flickering light of the candle his face looked hard, almost evil.

'I would like to speak with you for a moment, Comrade Prien.' I sat up.

'Go ahead.'

'I have come on account of the chap that pinched the ham,' he said.

'And what has that got to do with you?' I asked. 'And why doesn't he come himself?'

'He is howling,' he said briefly. Manthey was one of the oldest men there, nearly twenty-three, a miner from the Ruhr. He was a socialist, but one of the best workmen we had and always a good comrade.

'He told us that you have given him the sack,' he continued. 'I want to ask you to let him stay on.'

'I can't do that, the boy is a thief.'

'He pinched the ham,' replied Manthey sharply, 'because he needs money, because his mother is ill, and he wants to send her some cash.'

'Do you believe all that really?'

'Yes, I do,' he said emphatically.

Honestly I believed it, too. This miserable howling wretch was no common thief. That much human understanding I could claim to possess. And it was a good sign that Manthey was speaking on his behalf. But discipline had to be. I couldn't let it pass, much as I should like to have done for Manthey's sake.

'Look here, Comrade Manthey,' I said in as friendly a tone as possible, 'you must know that if I let this pass now then every son of a bitch can come along and say: "You shut your eyes that time when the ham was pinched, so why can't you do it with me?" And where are we then? No! The youngster must be punished and beside, imagine what sort of an impression would it make if people could say that the voluntary labour corp was a bunch of thieves?'

'I don't care a damn what they say outside,' he said roughly. 'You don't seem to consider what sort of an impression this is making on the boy. When the poor sod gets home, with his mother ill and his dad out of work and it gets about that he has come home because he is a thief, that won't be easy for him to cope with, I can tell you.'

I stood up. We were of equal height and looked each other straight in the eye.

'That is enough,' I said, 'my mind's made up, the matter is closed. And now go to bed.'

He stood there for a moment with compressed lips, then he turned about and left.

I was alone again.

For the first tirade I became conscious of the full force of the dilemma; on the one side the fate of the individual, on the other the weal of the community. I had decided for the latter, and I knew now that I should always decide in that sense, however hard it might be.

He was not at morning parade as I had seen to it that he left before duties started. I noticed that the columns looked discontented but I said nothing. I imagined they would come round in the end. I had not yet gathered sufficient experience in the handling of men and did not know that any opposition had to be nipped in the bud if one were not to be swamped by it.

When the columns returned in the evening there was warm meal waiting for them. I went into the dining hall when they were all at table. 'Good evening, comrades,' I said. Nobody replied. Conversation was hushed and at the same time feverish. They put their heads together and whispered and there would be sudden and brief laughter.

Suddenly a hoarse voice at the end of the table said aloud, 'We'll salt his ham for him.' I raised my head and looked in the direction from which the voice had come, but from where I stood it was impossible to say who had spoken. After dinner all of you parade in the schoolroom,' I commanded.

Instantly all were still. Then the whispers started again louder than before.

I sensed that here was the great test. If I failed they would have me in their power. That would be the end to all discipline in the camp. I knew I could not disappoint Lamprecht in such a way.

Half an hour later they were all assembled in the bar room where we held our meetings. It was November and outside it was already dark. In the wavering light of the candles shadows moved about on the white walls. I confronted them.

'Comrades, you all know what happened here. I was obliged to remove one from our midst because he was a thief. I know that many of you find this punishment too severe. But I had to be severe in the interests of us all'. There was a murmur on the benches at the back which grew from moment to moment. I paused for an instant. They continued to mutter. Then I bellowed as loud as I could, 'Those who don't like it can leave, at once.'

A scraping of feet. Someone stood up and then another and then they went out, thirty of them. Manthey was one of the first. I handed over to a group leader and followed the thirty.

'Fall in in the courtyard,' I commanded. They obeyed reluctantly.

'In half an hour from now you will have handed in your gear and left the camp. You don't belong to us any more. Anyone still here after that is trespassing. Dismiss.' Then I went back to the hall and informed the others. They received the news in silence. Nobody dared to make a comment. Then I went back to my cell. I felt miserable because I was sorry for the men who were leaving and for the end of a comradeship.

This was a regrettable incident but I had carried it through successfully and the work went on as before.

A few days later I heard that the Navy were giving commissions to officers of the Merchant Navy to bring the establishment up to strength. All the time I had longed to go back to the sea and now the longing gripped me irresistibly. Thus I joined the Navy in Stralsund in January 1933. Once again I began from the bottom as an ordinary sailor.

Eight
U-Boat Training

When a man joins the Forces he begins an entirely new life. Personal liberty is reduced to a minimum and its place is taken by the word of command, the iron discipline of service under arms. The sailor is always on duty. All personal experiences are reduced to unimportance compared with the service. This is expressed in an old saying: *Who swears his oath on the Prussian flag has nothing left that he can call his own.*

My naval training proceeded in this spirit. The service and the great political events overshadowed everything. After the conclusion of normal training I was posted to the U-Boats' training school at Kiel.

In the first few weeks of the course we were stuffed full to the back teeth with theory.

At last towards the end of February came the practical training, the day on which we went to sea for the first time in a U-Boat.

I can still clearly remember it all.

It was a clear windy day on which we sailed through *Kieler Forde,* the whole U-Boat flotilla in line ahead. Every boat carried a few officer aspirants. I was aboard the *U-3*.

When we arrived at the training area we climbed through the conning-tower hatch to the control room. In spite all our theoretical training we looked helplessly about the narrow room. Blinding white lights glinted in glass, nickel and brass, an inextricable network of electric cables compressed air conduits and pilot wheels surrounded us. In the centre was the periscope shaft and beside it the large main compass.

The noise of the diesel engines, which outside could be hardly heard above the noise of the sea, was here so loud that you couldn't hear yourself speak. Everything was vibrating. There was a penetrating smell of steel and oil.

The chief engineer received us. He inspected us with short sidelong glances and began his instruction. 'Never forget, gentlemen, to report off if you have to go on the upper deck when the boat is cleared for diving. Otherwise you will suffer the same fate as the legendary Lt Muller who found the boat sinking under his feet. If he hadn't had a bubble of air in his pants he would have drowned like a rat.'

A short word of command from the tower, 'Diving stations,' was answered from the stations by the reply, 'Foreship on diving station. Midship and aft'ship on diving stations.' Now the diving exercise began. Exhaust valves were closed and the hatch cover dropped into place with a metallic thud.

'Never forget to close the valves,' explained the chief engineer with a lowered voice, 'or you will have the same trouble the old *U-3* had in the Bay of Heikendorf. They also had officer aspirants on board and forgot to close the air inlet valves. Water streamed in and flooded the engine room. That caused a short circuit and filled the ship with deadly fumes. The commander was suffocated and most of the crew might have lost their lives, which would have been a pity. There were some pretty good fellows amongst them, Weddigen and Furbringer.'

A clear humming interrupted his words. The electric motors took over.

The hand-wheels turned and the fan began to spin.

Pressurization tests began. It felt as if the blood were rushing to the ears.

No one spoke; there was a continuous hum of machine and a spasmodic clatter of steering gear.

From the tower came back the order, 'Get ready flood tanks.'

'Tanks ready.'

'Flood tanks.'

Four men knelt and wrenched down the air levers. There was a hissing noise as the air escaped and the water gurgled into the tanks.

Slowly the boat inclined forward and then backward. There was a sensation of floating as in a balloon. Finally she came round on an even keel. It was deathly still. No one spoke, no one was allowed to move, only the C.E. gave his orders in a low voice to the men working the hydroplanes.

Then like a lift the periscope shot up.

One by one the Commander called us into the control room. For the first time I was going to see the world through a periscope. The horizon contracted to a small disc of sky and water which was flooded again and again by green waves.

Then we were shown how to manipulate the hydroplanes by means of large hand-wheels which one turned like coffee machines.

After we had been sailing submerged for a while the commander ordered. 'All stations! Boat descending to the bottom. Steer for the bottom, depth 21 metres.'

The C.E. reported '16...18...20 metres. Both engines stop.'

There was a slight jerk which shuddered through the whole boat and then we lay at rest upon the bottom of the sea. The C.E. reported, '22 metres diving depth, 2 tons downthrust'

Mess was at half past twelve. There was soup, rump steak and fruit for officers and crew. It was good and plentiful, but the wardroom was a little small, rather reminiscent of a tunnel. Occasionally the soft gurgle reminded us that we were 22 metres (or about 12 fathoms) down on the bottom of the Bay of Kiel.

From up aft came a sound as if somebody was working a handpump.

'What on earth is that?' asked Schreiber, one of the aspirants. The Commander remained silent but Number One grinned and said, 'He's using the lavatory. We hand pump all waste matter out. It's quite a job at 22 metres.'

His round face shone with pleasure for he enjoyed the topic, and he was not going to abandon it for some time. 'But that's nothing,' he continued briskly, 'just imagine, you are at war – then you have to control yourself for the sake of the Fatherland, for the stuff would float upward and give away the position of the boat.

'An old U-Boat man of the First World War told me a yarn about that. They were lying aground for 36 hours and then...'

'With a little effort we might perhaps find another topic of conversation,' suggested the Commander.

For two hours we remained on the sea bottom. Then the exercise continued. We ascended in stages, first to periscope depth and finally we surfaced. We were a little tired owing to the heavy atmosphere which was saturated with carbon dioxide and a little overcome by the rancid smell of the fuel oil.

Since that time I have done many trips under water and to be in a

U-Boat has become a commonplace for me. But the recollection of this first trip has remained vivid. Things and people are remembered most clearly when seen for the first or the last time.

At the conclusion of the training course I was posted as First Officer of the watch to *U-26*, under the command of Captain Lieutenant Hartmann. 'Sharp as a razor-blade,' remarked an old comrade, 'but you can learn a lot.'

The *U-26* was lying at Deschimag in Bremen. I broke my journey there at Hamburg and went out to *St Pauli* to visit Harry Stoewer, the old bo'sun of the *Hamburg* at the *Star of David*. I was always mindful of his help during my time of unemployment, when he gave me food and drink.

It was late in the afternoon. The *Star of David* was empty. An artificial blonde slouched behind the bar.

'Two large light ales and the landlord, please,' I ordered. She gazed at me in wonder, disappeared, and came back with a small thickset man buckling his trouser belt as he approached. It was not Harry Stoewer.

'What can I do for you, sir?' he asked.

'I want to find Harry Stoewer.'

'Sorry, sir,' he said regretfully, 'Harry Stoewer is dead; he died two years ago.' He turned as if to go.

'How did it happen?'

'He hanged himself,' said the landlord.

'Hanged himself? What on earth happened?' I pointed to the second glass.

The landlord nodded an acknowledgement and sat down.

'Well, you know old Stoewer wasn't a business man. He lent to everybody on the security of their blue eyes. And at the end he had hardly anything to eat himself. A business like this has to be learnt, you know. People think all you have to do is to stand behind the bar and dish out beer.'

I thanked him and went.

All the way to the station I thought of Harry Stoewer.

I asked myself why he had not turned to his friends for help.

He had helped so many others and yet when he was in need of help himself he just hanged himself. He had been happy to be of assistance to anybody and too good-hearted to keep afloat in this harsh world of shopkeepers and profiteers.

I went on by the next train, and when I arrived in Bremen I went straight out to the shipyard. The boat lay close to the quay, moored to a buoy. From the height of the quay it looked very small.

I climbed down and reported to the Commander who received me in his cabin. He was a thickset, but wiry man with a hard and clear-cut face.

'Lieutenant Prien begs to report for duty in *U-26*.' He rose and shook me by the hand.

'Well, here you are, I have been expecting you. But at the moment there is nothing here that you can do. Haven't you still got a spot of leave coming?' I grasped the situation at once. 'Yes, sir,' I said.

'Very well then, push off for a week.' I thanked him and left at once.

It seemed these days as if the past were catching up with me. On my way home I met an ensign. We got into conversation and he showed me a photograph of a group at a New Year's ball.

Amongst all the unknown faces I spotted one that was familiar, the fair girl of the garden in Plauen to whom I had given the kiss and the roses. The memory of the incident was still fresh in my mind.

I asked the ensign to give me her address, and wrote to her.

Her reply soon arrived.

She thanked me for my letter which she had found very amusing. But she claimed that she had never been to Plauen. Six months later we were married and I have never regretted it since. So much for romance.

My leave was cut short. Three days later I was called back by telegram.

'We are going to Spain,' said the Commander when we met. 'Just to guard German interests.' His face was beaming with joy.

The boat was quickly placed on a war footing; store, fuel and munitions were taken on board and we left the very next day. All of us believed that the heat would be oppressive on that occasion but the thunder passed close by and the lightening struck on land.

In the canal we did a trim dive. I was in the control room. The station reported: 'Clear for diving'; the torpedo crew reported, 'Clear'. Then came the command 'Submerge'.

Then a sudden cry from the torpedo hatch, 'The fish, the fish.' I ran forrard. A torpedo had slipped back out of its tube and was protruding into the hatch. Four men, gasping with exertion, were trying to push it back.

It was clear that they would not be able to hold much longer. The weight of the torpedo forced them step by step. If the stern of the boat should drop by only a few degrees, the projectile would slide into the hatch, crush the men and tear the boat to pieces.

I rushed aft. 'Fish sliding backward,' I yelled to the C.E.

He understood. The hand-wheels of the hydroplane began to hum.

Running back forrard I pushed with all my weight against the torpedo. Slowly the boat swung back on even keel and equally slowly, inch by inch, the fish slid back into the tube until at last the lock closed behind it with a metallic ring.

'How did it happen?' I demanded. The Petty Officer stood in front of me, wet with perspiration and trembling all over. The veins on his forehead stood out like ropes.

'I don't know, sir,' he gasped, 'I cleared the torpedo and closed the lock and I suppose a bolt must have jammed.'

'So you reported 'All Clear for diving', prematurely?'

He compressed his lips. 'Yes, sir,' he said in an undertone.

After I had reported to the Commander he sent for the Petty Officer and gave him the dressing down of his life.

At breakfast later on he said calmly and apparently quite unconcerned, 'It would have been just one of those things; anyhow a U-Boat isn't an old age insurance.'

There were plenty of incidents on this voyage. In the Bay of Biscay we ran into as heavy a storm as I was ever to experience on a U-Boat. When at eight bells I went on to the bridge, wrapped in heavy oilskins, the sky was leaden and the sea as black as ink. The boat ploughed through the hissing waves, as the pelting rain whipped across our faces. From time to time the seas broke over the ship and we stood waist deep in icy water.

That was just the beginning. The seas rose above us, higher and more threatening, dark but mottled with shreds of spume, and then they crashed down upon us with the force of a cataract. Safety belts were brought up and we fastened ourselves to the rail. All save the Commander. He stood in front on the conning tower, his hands clutching the rail and with his head lowered he seemed to be attacking the waves like a bull.

The diesel engines laboured. Every time we were carried on the crest of a wave the screws threshed the air. A glassy wall of water rose in front of us higher than any before, then we disappeared under the water. As we came up again spitting and coughing one man was missing; the Petty Officer of the bridge. The fastenings off his belt had broken, and he was draped over the rail of the tower like a wet bathing suit. In one jump the Commander was upon him and had wrenched him back. He was sent below with two other men and we remained alone on the tower.

The seas increased in height. At times they were so tall that only the heads of the men on the bridge showed above the water. At last we had no other choice but to dive. During the next lull we ducked through the conning tower hatch. A flood of water poured down behind us into the boat. The bilge pumps began to splutter and finally we submerged.

The lower we went the quieter it became until nothing could be heard of the outer world but the noises of the boat and the high whine of the electric engines.

For many hours we continued under water and when we surfaced again, the storm was over.

In front of us, the Spanish coast rose steep and dark into the grey of the morning. No lights could be seen; only the moon shone through the tattered clouds.

The navigator cursed. Without sea marks it was impossible to fix our position. All he could say was that we lay somewhere between Bilbao and Santander.

We started our patrol, cruising to and fro between Pesajas and Cape Finisterre. The sea was empty, though occasionally we sighted some plumes of smoke over the, horizon. The land lay dark and silent. Only when the wind was off shore were we able to hear distant gunfire. The sound got into our blood and aroused the desire felt by every true soldier, to be in on the fighting. But the time was not yet ripe.

Once only did war pass us by so closely that we felt sure we would be drawn into it. That was in front of Bilbao.

The lookout called, 'Two warships on the port bow.' The Commander and I went on the bridge. We recognised the cruiser *Almirante Cerdeira* and the destroyer *Belastro,* Franco's ships, steaming at full speed towards us, huge waves foaming at their bows. Studying them through our glasses we saw their guns slowly turning towards us.

'They probably take us for a Republican boat,' said the Commander.

It was a sticky situation. I glanced at Hartmann. What was he going to do? If we altered course they would take it for retreat and fire upon us. If we went to meet them they would take it as an attack. If we dived they would rain depth charges down upon us.

'Stop both engines,' ordered the Commander. We hove to and lay rolling in the swell. We hoisted our ensign at the wireless mast and our searchlight signalled at three-second intervals. *Aleman, Aleman, Aleman.*

In vain; they continued to advance.

'Getting a bit hot here,' I said, running my finger round my collar.

The commander laughed.

The muzzles of their guns were now pointed directly at us, but when they were about a mile and a half away they turned away and their guns swung back to the normal position. They steamed past and dipped their flags in salute.

Nine
The First Sharp Rounds

I received my first command in the autumn of 1938. At last I was captain of my own ship.

I went to Kiel in December and looked up Captain Lieutenant Sobe, Chief of the Flotilla, in his quarters in the depot ship *Hamburg*. He received me in his cabin.

'Have you been across the yard and looked at your boat?'

'Not yet, sir.'

He smiled, while his shrewd grey eyes weighed me up.

'Have you inspected your crew?'

'No, sir.'

'Well, then you had better go and have a look at both. We shook hands, barked, '*Heil* Hitler', to each other and parted.

My ship was still lying in the yard receiving its final touches. She was a beautiful boat with lovely lines. I went aboard and, bursting with the pride of possession, inspected every single thing from stem to stern.

I went to the First Lieutenant and ordered him to Commander's inspection for ten o'clock next morning.

The following day was clear and sunny. Climbing the ladder to the quarterdeck I felt a curious sense of excitement at the thought of meeting my crew for the first time. Standing out there on deck were the thirty-eight men with whom I was to share my life for the next few years whether good or bad, in peace, or, if it had to be, in war.

I saw them standing in two ranks with their officers and non-commissioned officers. A sharp word of command, "Shun! Eyes left.'

The officer-in-charge approached me and said, 'First Lieutenant Wessels begs to report crew present and correct.' He was a broad-shouldered man with a heavy and serious face. I stepped forward, cried, '*Heil* Hitler', and the reply roared back, '*Heil* Hitler'.

I had often wondered what I should say to the men of my first command. But now as I stood before them I said simply: 'In a few days we shall be a new unit of the German Navy. I look to everyone to do his duty as I shall do mine. If we all do that we shall get on all right.'

I went along the line asking the name and grade of each member of the crew. They were mostly fresh young faces, as yet unmarked by life. A few faces impressed themselves on me. There was Endrass, the First Officer, small, sporty; Spahr, the navigator, heavy and self-possessed; there was the broad good-humoured face of Gustav Bohm, the chief engine-room artificer; the curiously withdrawn look in the eyes of the engineer's mate Holstein; the shrewd Smyczek and the open and fresh countenance of Ludecke. I spoke with them all and tried to find out what sort of men they were. But at the best it was only guesswork, for the qualities of men do not emerge except in danger and at work.

In the following spring we had daily trial runs with the boat, first in the bay and then in the Baltic Sea. I began to get to know my men. Certainly they were no parade-ground soldiers, but they had their hearts in the right place, filled with the spirit of adventure and full of zest which they showed at every opportunity. They were all volunteers and expected a more interesting life in the U-Boat service than they might have had on a battleship.

Early in August we sailed into the Atlantic on large-scale manoeuvres. International tension was running high and there were many who expected war by the time we returned.

The manoeuvres were most successful. We had excellent weather, clear summer days with a low swell and starlit nights. Whenever possible we listened to broadcasts from home. It gave one a pleasantly queer feeling to hear the voice of the broadcaster coming across thousands of miles.

But the news was serious and smelled of war. The exercise that we had begun with such enthusiasm had become meaningless and it was easy to see the men were slacking off. The watches below lay around in their bunks and discussed politics. Gustav Bohm was tireless and his words were imbued with profound wisdom.

But at the bottom of our hearts we did not believe in the possibility of war – or, at least not a great war, for the thought of nations being at each others throats again seemed too incredible.

And then war came.

I remember the hour as if it were yesterday. I was standing on the tower with Endrass at about ten o'clock on that September morning. Brisk nor'westerly winds were blowing, and the waves were capped with foam. The boat was running half speed and from the ship came the deep soothing hum of the engines.

A voice cried up from below, 'Sir, sir,' and was followed by the appearance of Hansel through the conning-tower hatch. His face was pale and he stuttered breathlessly so that the words ran into each other, 'Signal, sir. War with England, sir.'

I rushed down the ladder. Down below in the control-room Spahr and two other men were standing in front the little brown box from which military marches coming in a quick and exciting rhythm. They stood silently with stern faces. 'What is it?' I demanded.

'They are going to repeat, sir,' whispered Spahr. The music stopped and the voice of the announcer came through. 'This is the German Rundfunk. Here is a special announcement. 'The British Government has addressed an ultimatum to the German Government demanding the withdrawal of the German troops now on Polish territory. This morning at nine o'clock the British Ambassador in Berlin has presented an insolent note informing the German Government that unless a satisfactory reply was received in London by eleven o'clock this morning, Great Britain would consider herself as being at war with Germany. The British Ambassador has been informed that the Government and the German people decline to accept or fulfil any demands contained in a British ultimatum!'

This was followed by the reading of the German memorandum. Then there was another march.

We were silent. Thoughts passed through my mind in rapid succession.

War: the taking of a prize; the free choice of a field of a field of operation.

The marches were still sounding through the ship. It was as if everyone was waiting with bated breath for what was to be. The three men in the control-room stared at me. I turned to the chart-table, beckoning Spahr to join me.

'Lay the course on 220 degrees. Here is where we shall operate from,' I said pointing to a place on the chart.

Unconsciously I had lowered my voice. From the ward-room forrard where the watch below had gathered came a voice, 'God have mercy on those who started it.'

Slowly I climbed up into the tower. Endrass and the two sentries looked tensely at me.

'Well, Endrass, this is it,' I said.

'Well then, let's do our best,' he said bravely.

Then I issued my orders. 'All lookout posts are constantly to use their glasses. Report as soon as anything is sighted. Pay particular attention to planes and periscopes of hostile U-Boats.'

Endrass saluted and I went below again. In the little hutch which served me as a sleeping and rest room I began on the first page of my war diary.

When I had finished the entry I crawled into my bunk, thought to myself that this was to be our testing time, and as I realized that I needed all my strength I decided to sleep, while there was still a chance.

I was awakened by a shout, 'Bridge to Commander Smoke on the starboard bow.' I jumped up. Someone in the control-room repeated the message. I grabbed my cap and went up to the tower. Far away in the pale afternoon sky was a plume of smoke, thin and unsteady like a very distant bonfire. I took up my glasses and focused them on the smoke.

Very slowly a minute black spot edged over the horizon. We set our course towards the ship and I ordered, 'Full speed ahead.' The spume of the bow wave blew over deck. Gradually we neared the ship which appeared to a freighter of between 5,000 to 6,000 tons. As soon as we could sight the blunt superstructure of the bridge we submerged.

The diesel engines were cut. Water rushed into the tanks and in a high whine the electric motors took over. We stood in the control-room. Eyes glued to the periscope stared at the black spot which gradually moved towards us. Endrass called up, 'Is that one?'

'Keep quiet, man,' I said, 'wait till daddy's had a look.'

We placed ourselves directly in the course of the approaching ship and were moving straight towards her. I could recognise her nationality. She was a Greek freighter, old and dirty, dragging her cargo laboriously over the sea.

'A Greek,' I said aloud and then added, 'get ready for action, prepare signal flags, report when ready.' The sound of steps came from below, followed by the rattling noise made by shells being taken out of their cradles and the metallic click when they were stacked ready for use. A few moments later every station reported, 'All clear for action.'

We blew five tanks and surfaced.

The conning-tower hatch swung open and we dashed on to the bridge. Behind me the gun crew swarmed up the ladder.

'Fire a round ahead of her,' I ordered.

The gun barked sharply. The echo of the detonation rang through the boat. The shell struck a hundred yards in front of the ship, a geyser sprung up and a cloud of gunsmoke drifted over the water.

While the aerial mast was being set up Endrass ordered, 'Reload.'

The deck of the ship looked like a disturbed anthill.

With our glasses we could clearly see the crew running aimlessly about. Our appearance had given them the fright of their lives,

Slowly the ship stopped and lay wallowing in the swell and blowing off steam while the Greek national flag was broken at the mast

We signalled back, 'Send a boat over with your papers.' Cautiously we approached the old vessel, our gun ready to fire if need be.

We were now within hailing distance. Through the megaphone I called across, 'Send a boat please with your papers.' In the instant that I raised my megaphone the heads disappeared behind the bulwark and only the hands were visible in what looked like a German salute. After a while a voice called from the ship, 'OK, sir.'

Feverish activity broke out on board, the two lifeboats were swung out and the crew climbed in with ape-like agility. Hatch covers, fenders, and boards flew overboard. No sooner had the boats touched water than the crew pulled madly at the oars sending them away from us and away from their own ship. It seemed as though they were rowing in a regatta, so rapidly were they trying to get away from us. Slowly we followed and drew level with them after a few minutes. The crew immediately shipped their oars and reached high above their heads.

'Where is the Captain?' I asked.

A tall fair man got up from athwart.

'Your papers?'

With a shaking hand he offered us the brown briefcase. I examined the papers carefully. Everything was in perfect order. It was a neutral ship carrying cargo to – Germany.

There wasn't the slightest reason for all this fuss.

'All right,' I said and returned his brief case, 'you go on.' He looked at me incredulously.

'You must not wireless your encounter with me,' I told him, 'that would be a hostile act.'

Nodding his head he raised his arm in the German salute. We cast off and proceeded on our way, the men in the boats remained glued to their seats with upraised arms, as if turned to stone. We were nearly a mile away before they rowed back to the abandoned ship.

'I hope he hasn't put us in the shit, sir,' said Gustav Bohm, his moon face registering deep concern.

Thereupon I answered quietly, 'My dear Gustav, in the first place as an old merchant skipper I can see quite well without spectacles and secondly, a Christian like you should use that word only in the most exceptional circumstances.'

He clicked his heels so that his fat little cheeks quivered. Astern of us the Greek freighter was disappearing over the horizon.

We continued on our course along the main sea lane. But since our first encounter we were dogged by ill luck for we saw nothing but sky and water for the next few days.

At last, early in the morning of the fifth of September, we sighted another plume of smoke.

I happened to be on the bridge. A light mist lay over the waves and beyond, the sun rose, blood red.

It was difficult to see clearly in the half-light. By the time we had sighted the smoke, the ship had already come over the horizon. She was steering a curious zig-zag course like a dragon fly flitting over a stream.

Endrass remarked, 'She seems to have a bad conscience.'

We dived. I stood at the periscope and watched the ship approach. She was a short and dumpy freighter painted in weird colours. The stack was a flaming red, the super-structure black and the bottom grass green. On the bows *Bosnia* was painted in large letters.

The English merchantman had obviously been warned and was prepared for the worst. It would have been a mistake to surface in front of her as she was possibly armed or might be tempted to ram us. So I let the ship go past and we surfaced a short distance astern and fired a shot over her. The ship altered course and turned stern to us and I noticed the foam of the propeller swirling up. She was trying to escape. We fired a second round, this time so close that the column of water splashed on deck. But she refused to stop. At the same time my signaller sang out; 'Signal to Commander: Enemy sending radio messages.'

A runner came hurrying up the ladder. 'Here is the intercepted message, sir.' He gave me the slip of paper: *Under attack and fire from German U-Boat. Urgently require assistance.* Here followed his position and the message ended with *SOS, SOS, SOS.*

That settled it. I gave Endrass a sign. Swiftly and with precision the crew loaded the gun. Then Endrass barked 'Fire.' A sharp report and the *Bosnia* was hit amidships. A cloud of smoke rose up, but still the *Bosnia* continued her flight.

'Five rounds rapid fire,' I ordered.

Again we could clearly see the second shell hit its target then the third.

At last the ship hove to and lay there like a wounded animal. From the hold heavy blue and yellow smoke belched up and formed a column over the ship like a pine tree swaying in the wind. The cargo must have included a large quantity of sulphur. We closed in on the *Bosnia,* as the crew rustled to the boats and launched them.

Hansel sang out behind me. 'Column of smoke in sight.' I turned about. On the north-west horizon appeared a thick streak of smoke, heavy and black, like a mourning flag. Swiftly I considered my situation. It could be a destroyer coming to the aid of the freighter.

'Keep that ship well in sight,' I told Hansel, 'and report at once if you can see what her nationality is.'

The crew of the *Bosnia* had been over hasty in their efforts to escape. One boat had filled with water and was foundering. It was pathetic to see the men drift helplessly away. Some of them shouted for help while others beckoned to us. We steered towards the sinking boat. Samann and Dittmer reached down to help the floating men aboard leaning far overboard so that their hands nearly touched the water.

By now the lifeboat of the *Bosnia* had filled with water and the sea swept over it. A few heads were floating close together, then a wave separated them. In the space of a few seconds only a handful were left.

A few non-swimmers threshed about with their arms. Others were swimming with long strokes towards sea-worthy lifeboat of the *Bosnia,* which had turned towards the men in the water.

Reaching out Dittmer and Samann grabbed one of the men and heaved him on board. He was a small red-headed boy, probably the mess-boy. He sat up gasping, while water was running down his face and dripping from his clothes.

Behind me Hansel reported, 'It is a Norwegian freighter, sir.' I turned round and took up the glasses. The ship that was coming up from the sou'west lay high; apparently she had no cargo on board.

'OK Hansel,' I said and heaved a sigh of relief. I would not have welcomed an encounter with a destroyer before I had sunk the *Bosnia.*

In the meantime the boy recovered his breath, got up and stepped to the rail beside Dittmer.

He was shivering with fright. I beckoned him to the bridge.

Are you the mess-boy?' I asked.

'Yes, sir.'

'What was your cargo?'

'Sulphur, sir.'

'Where were you bound for?'

'Glasgow.'

He spoke in a cockney accent but his answers were completely unselfconscious. He was a boy from the London slums, a type of person who is impressed by no one and nothing.

'You are trembling. Are you afraid?'

He shook his head. 'No. I'm only cold, sir.'

'You will have a spot of brandy later on,' I said. He nodded his head and added, perhaps to show his gratitude, 'Of course, we got a fright, sir, you can't imagine what it's like; you looks over the water and sees nothing, on'y sky and water and then suddenly a bloomin' big thing pops up beside yer, blowing like a walrus. I thought I was seein' the Loch Ness monster.'

We approached the second boat of the *Bosnia*.

'Where is your Captain?' I called over the water.

An officer stood up and pointed to the *Bosnia*.

'He is on board,' he said.

I gazed at the ship which was wreathed in clouds of smoke and flaming like a volcano.

'What is he doing there?'

'He is burning his documents.'

I understood. There was a man alone on the burning ship, hundreds of miles from land and without a lifeboat, destroying his ship's papers lest they fall into the hands of the enemy. I had to admire his courage.

'And who are you?' I asked the officer.

He raised his hand to his cap, 'I am the First Officer of the *Bosnia*.'

'Come aboard.'

Dittmer helped him to climb on board. On the whole he did not look very much like a seaman; pale; fat and tired. When he stood on the deck he saluted again.

In the meantime the little mess-boy had been taken on board the other lifeboat of the *Bosnia* and we steered towards the new arrival, the large Norwegian vessel which floated almost completely out of water.

On our way we came across one of the shipwrecked men and while we stopped Samann and Dittmer hauled him on board.

I came down from the tower to have a look at the man they had brought up. He lay there lifeless, a small skinny man still fairly young in years, but worn out like an old horse. There were traces of coal dust on his clothes. He had probably been a stoker on board the *Bosnia*.

Samann had removed his jacket and shirt; the fellow was painfully thin and his ribs showed up clearly like the bars of a cage.

Dittmer grasped him by the arms and began artificial respiration.

The First Officer of the *Bosnia* was standing beside be. Looking down at the man he said abruptly, 'You Germans are good-hearted people, sir.'

I looked at him standing there, fat, well-fed and probably mighty satisfied with himself.

I could not contain myself and said gruffly, 'It would have been better if you people had given that poor fellow something to eat in your ship.' Leaving him standing there I returned to the tower.

The Norwegian vessel had now approached so close by that her large national flag flying from the fore-mast was clearly visible. I flagged her to stop and she hove to, so close to our boat that the sides towered over us like a cliff.

We signalled, 'Please take crew of English ship on board.'

The Norwegian ship replied, 'Ready.' A boat was lowered and when it came alongside, the little stoker, still unconscious, was put aboard first, followed by the First Officer who saluted once more before he left.

I talked with the officer-in-charge of the Norwegian lifeboat, and explained the situation to him. I pointed to the *Bosnia's* lifeboat, with the *Bosnia* burning close beside. Just then a man on board the *Bosnia* jumped into the water, probably the Captain who had managed to destroy his papers.

I pointed towards him and said, 'You must save that man also.' The Norwegian officer nodded and cast off.

We waited until they had finished the rescue work. It took quite a time, while our lookouts nervously scanned the horizon; the *Bosnia* had wirelessed for help and her cloud of smoke stood like a huge pillar over the burning ship which must have been visible for hundreds of miles.

At last the Norwegian vessel dipped her flag and steamed off.

We were obliged to sacrifice a torpedo to finish off the *Bosnia*.

It was our first torpedo release and everyone wanted to observe its effect. So, nearly the whole crew came on deck. We had of course seen from photographs from the First World War how the stricken steamer appears to rear up in the water and then swiftly slide to the bottom.

But this was quite different, much less showy and all the more impressive because of that. There was a dull explosion and huge columns of water rose up high the mast. And then the stricken ship simply broke in two pieces which in a space of seconds disappeared into the sea. A few bits of driftwood and the empty boats were all that was left.

We steamed briskly to the north but did not encounter our next ship until two days later. It was an English ship again, a freighter of about 3,000 tons, the name was the *Gartavon*, written in large white letters on her sides. We surfaced close astern and sent a shot across her bows. She refused to stop and wirelessed for help.

Our second shot silenced the radio. The crew took to the boats. It was wonderful to see how efficiently they carried out this task. There was no confusion and not one false move. In fact it was smarter than I have seen on some naval exercises.

I thought appreciatively that there was very good discipline on that ship. As soon as the boats were afloat the crew began to pull off with brisk regular strokes. When they were some distance away they stepped masts and set sail. I watched this through the glasses. It was beautifully carried out. Then I turned towards the ship. My blood froze. The crewless *Gartavon* was steaming in an arc straight towards us. Before leaving the ship the crew had started the engines and set the course of the ship in our direction in the hope that we would be cut in half by it.

'Engines full speed ahead,' I shouted.

Those were very unpleasant moments before the engines of our U-Boat sprang to life.

The *Gartavon* came very close, the shadow of her rigging swept over our deck.

At last the water began to swirl under our propellers and we shot forward. Behind us the steamer cut through our wake so close that the bow wave forced our stern round.

A cold fury gripped me. We made after the two lifeboats that were rapidly drawing away from us. They were sailing and rowing at the same time in an endeavour to escape. While we were chasing them I kept saying to myself, 'Don't forget that these people are shipwrecked.'

When we reached the Captain's boat we stopped, barely ten yards away. I grasped the megaphone and called

'Captain, ahoy.'

A slim and fair man stood up in the stern. He was the Captain of the *Gartavon*, very correct and very well turned out, an officer from tip to toe. Beside him on the thwart sat the Chief Engineer. White teeth gleamed through his dark beard. I was certain it was he who, with the consent of the Captain, had set his ship to ram us.

'Have you still any hands on board?' I called through my megaphone.

The Captain cupped his hands to his mouth.

He replied, 'No, sir.'

'Since you have committed a hostile act I shall not radio for you but I will send you the next neutral ship I meet.'

He remained calm. 'OK, sir,' and after a short pause, 'May I proceed?'

Yes,' I called back, 'you may.'

He gave a salute which I acknowledged.

We were very polite to each other, like knightly opponents in a novel. But behind this formality lay an icy hatred, the hatred of two peoples who are facing other in the last decisive round. We went back to *Gartavon* which was still steaming round in circles. To save torpedoes we sent a few shells into the hull. The side gaped open, white steam belched forth and slowly the *Gartavon* settled deeper in the water. We fired another shot. Clumsily as an animal that is mortally wounded the ship on her side and rolled over. For a moment the keel showed green with seaweed and then she sank.

From then on the war hardened with every day. The British began to arm their merchant ships and send then in convoys. We acted accordingly. Every vessel in an enemy convoy was liable to be torpedoed without warning and we worked according to the formula: *Any ship in convoy to the bottom.*

So far I had not encountered a convoy, but late one afternoon in the winter we observed, while submerged, a plume of smoke rising above the grey horizon. Then we saw the rigging of a large ship and behind it another one, and finally, a forest of masts seemed to steam towards us. We counted twelve steamers guarded by five British destroyers. In evasive action the large ships steamed from side to side like drunkards crossing a street, while the small destroyers circled in zig-zags around them.

We made directly towards them. The sea was fairly rough and a low grey cloud hung over the water. The wind blew from the nor'west directly towards us. It was not east to follow the movements of the enemy and again and again I had to change my course.

Green water washed over the periscope we had pushed cautiously and this impeded observation. Moreover, the light was failing.

At last night fell and sky and sea faded to a uniform grey. I gazed at the flock of ships and closed in on the prey I had selected, a tubby tanker the third in the row. It was larger and heavier than any of the other ships and moreover a tanker is very valuable. Nor had we forgotten Earl Jellicoe's saying in the last war that the Allies had floated to victory on a wave of oil. At least this wave would not reach the shore. We were now so close that we had to slow down so as not to ram the ship. We could clearly hear the heavy throbbing of her engines. In the image of the periscope her bows came into view. A huge black wall was rising up in front of the sky and finally filled the whole view.

'Torpedo one – Fire,' I commanded. The recoil of the fish shuddered through the boat. Down below Spahr was chanting in a steady voice: 13…14…15… it wasn't possible that we should have missed at this short range…16…something was certainly wrong. I found what it was. I had forgotten to change the magnification of the periscope! At the same moment there was a dull detonation. Three cheers, for the fish had landed.

Cautiously the periscope was pushed up. There was a blinding light and a huge column of flame was surging up to the sky out of the hold of the tanker.

Two destroyers swept down towards us.

'Attention, destroyers,' I yelled. Already the first depth charges were blowing the sea up with an ear-splitting *EEyoooom!* We felt the concussion in the ship.

The periscope was lowered and we turned tail. There was a breathless pause and then closer, the second series of charges went off. It was as if the boat lay in the grip of a giant fist that shook to and fro. Then again silence. Through the firing, we could hear the propellers of the approaching destroyers, a nerve-racking sound.

Then came the third series of charges.

This time the invisible fist struck us a fearful blow. There was a shattering of glass, an eerie half-light as the bulbs exploded. The gauges jumped wildly and the splinters flew.

The boat rocked like a boxer out on his feet. Through it came Wessel's calm voice, 'Report damage to control-room.'

From the stations came back the answers, 'Aft – three bulbs broken.'

'Forrard quarters two manometers defective, bulbs broken.'

'Wireless room, light fused, emergency lighting now in use.'

Then a sound as if a sealion was blowing air and then a voice from the control-room, 'Damme, we've got away with it.'

We were drawing away. The noise of the next lot of charges sounded far behind us.

But suddenly from in front of us came the sound of detonation as though steel was being wrenched apart. Slowly we pushed up our periscope. It was now full night. Against the dark sky there rose a huge dome of fire 1,500 feet long and 300 feet high.

The tanker had blown up and spilled its burning contents over the sea. For a second the thought of the men in this flaming hell passed through my mind, and I shuddered.

Ten
In Trouble

We had orders to prevent the landing of British troops and for days we had been cruising in the vicinity of Narvik. One April afternoon we ran into the fjord. It was a bright day, the sun shining out of a pale blue sky and the snow-clad mountains reflecting the brilliant light.

Cautiously we crept up the fjord. On either side sheer walls of rock hundreds of feet high dropped almost vertically to the sea. In front of us lay the narrow fairway, dark and quiet. It was very uncomfortable, for at any moment a hostile aircraft might appear and in the clear water we were visible at a great depth. Any of the crevices in the cliff face could conceal a foe, ready to pounce and destroy us, just as we were ready to destroy him. Every house and every street threatened danger, for at this time Norway's attitude was still undecided.

We stood on the bridge and carefully searched sky, sea and land with our glasses. Observing a small settlement of tiny brown huts clinging to the hillside, we went down to periscope depth.

When we surfaced again it was night. The pale bright summer night of the North, where only colour fades but contours remain clear.

Slowly the boat crept round a promontory. Close in front of us, barely 200 metres away, a warship was lying at anchor, clearly silhouetted against the white snow of the hills. It was a British cruiser of between 7,000 and 8,000 tons. At once I prepared our boat for attack. We were already nearing the end of our patrol and there was only one torpedo left in the forrard tube. Only one shot which simply had to connect.

'Get ready… Stand by to fire… Fire!'

The shock of the recoil was still vibrating through the ship as we turned away. We had to turn slowly and carefully because at speed the bow wave and the noise of the engines would have betrayed our position, so close were we to our opponent, whilst it was impossible to dive close to shore. While the boat turned we watched the path of the torpedo.

'Damn and blast it, a dud!' The torpedo was deviating from its course and curving towards the rocky cliff in front of the warship.

Suddenly there was a scraping noise under our keel and we had stuck fast, right under the guns of the enemy. At the same moment the torpedo hit the rock with a tremendous explosion and a column of water shot up the wall of the cliff.

For a fraction of a second I thought that all was lost. If we wanted to get away we had to work fast

'Both engines full speed astern,' I roared.

The engines sprang into action. Sparks flew and thick fumes belched from the exhaust in the stern, but the boat did not budge. I glanced across to the cruiser. There was nothing to be seen. There she lay, dark and silent like a sleeping monster. I grabbed Number One. 'Go and wake the free watch. Tell them to run from side to side and rock the ship.'

I ordered the Second Officer below to destroy all papers, and set charges to blow up the boat in case we fell into enemy's hands. He vanished through the hatch.

I looked at the cruiser. It was incredible but she still showed no sign of life. I thought to myself that I would like to be able to sleep like that when I was pensioned off. 'Drain water from torpedo tubes and pressure tanks,' I ordered, for it was essential to lighten the ship forrard.

There was feverish activity. Men swarmed up from below, stumbling in their haste, ran down past me on to the deck. A short blast from the whistle of the First Officer and there was a stamping of many feet.

The crew ran to port. Again a muted blast of the whistle, hardly audible above the noise of the engines, and the feet stamped across to starboard. And so it went on for many minutes, over – back – and over and back again and again. The vessel moved slightly but did not free herself. I tried to turn, so I ordered the starboard engine to stop, then the rudder aport and starboard engine half-speed forrard. We turned terribly slowly and clumsily but still we remained stuck fast

The port lookout came up to me and whispered, 'Sir, over there! Something is moving.'

Where?' I exclaimed.

He pointed into the night.

In the fjord, in front of our bay, a vessel was slowly moving towards us, soundlessly and barely visible, grey in the grey night.

Then lights appeared, morse signals calling us and giving recognition signs.

'Shall I make a reply, Sir?' the signaller asked in a low voice although the noise of the engines drowned all speech

We had now two enemies to cope with, at our back the cruiser, and in front another enemy ship.

Hansel held the morse lamp ready.

'Leave that,' I said quickly. 'Perhaps he thinks we are a blacked out markship.'

He was still blinking morse at us but we did not reply and finally he abandoned his signals.

Hansel turned to me.

'Sir,' he said, 'over there is an old fishing cutter.' He broke off, but in this moment of tension our minds were so attuned that I understood him without further words. If everything went wrong we could perhaps get to Narvik in her, I thought, and called down into the control-room.

'Bring up machine guns, grenades and ammo.' I glanced over to the cruiser which was still asleep.

The port lookout reported, 'Sir, that's a trawler.'

I looked closely and indeed he was right; an armed trawler had come to rest at the entrance of our bay. We were trapped and helpless, without a torpedo; a sitting target for two opponents either of whom was more powerful than we were.

The voice of the navigator came across, 'Boat is moving astern,' and at the same moment we heard a crunching noise; the boat lurched hard astern, heeled to port and rocked to an even keel.

Thank God! We were free!

'All men, except bridge watch, below deck,' I commanded. 'Prepare to dive.'

We slowly advanced towards the trawler which was blocking our way. Barely a thousand yards from him we dived and passed under him and by the time he had spotted us we were already out of the fjord. Behind us sounded the angry explosions of his depth charges.

When I got to the control-room I heard a man say, 'Well, that was close shave.'

And I thought that if I had had time I should certainly have had the wind up!

Eleven
66,000 Tons

It was two o'clock in the morning, I was lying on my bunk in a restless half-sleep. From the radio room opposite came the pip, pip, peep of the morse transmitter, quite close to my ear and only separated by a baize curtain. It was rather a tight fit on board.

Steinhagen reported, 'Sir, radio signal to all boats received, German aircraft shot down in North Sea,' and gave the exact position.

I jumped out of my bunk, grabbed my cap and went over to the control-room. Casting a rapid glance at the chart I saw that the indicated position lay close to our course. I climbed on to the tower. The bridge watch stood wrapped in their greatcoats for it was a piercingly dry cold that morning.

I gave brief directions to the watch of the bridge, 'Keep a sharp lookout for aircraft wreckage,' then I went back to the control, indicated the new course and left orders to be called at seven o'clock unless anything unexpected happened before.

Sharp at seven I was awakened by Roth switching on the light above my head. When I got on to the bridge the early morning mist was drifting in swathes over the water. Nothing had been seen of the aircraft and nothing else had occurred during my sleep.

It was rotten luck, for we had already passed the indicated position where the crew of the aircraft were drifting helplessly in the sea.

Deep in thought, I went to the wardroom where Barendorff was already at breakfast. We were sitting opposite each other, hemmed in by lockers and bunks. Barendorff said something. I hardly heard him, for my thoughts were still with the helpless airmen. We had to get to them somehow. I had an inspiration. Jumping up I rushed the control-room and called up to the bridge, 'Hard aport. New course 245 degrees.' I returned to the table. Barendorff gave me a sidelong glance but said nothing. Then he got up and went on to the bridge. I continued my breakfast

A message came from the bridge: 'Lights ahead.'

I climbed on to the tower.

Barendorff pointed ahead into, the mist, 'I saw a white light just over there.' We approached the spot; a round dark object was floating on the waves – a floating mine – we circled it and then in front of us spotted a dark grey shape which was drifting towards us. It was a collapsable boat with three men on board.

A few of the crew were standing at the rail to watch proceedings. They were excited and jubilant. 'Boy, oh boy,' bo'sun called out in his trumpet-like voice. 'Are those chaps going to be pleased?'

An answering shout came from the dinghy. Two men jumped up and waved their arms and shouted, throwing their hats above their heads.

We slowly manoeuvred alongside the dinghy. The airmen had stopped rowing and in their joy they nearly forgot to catch the line we had thrown to them. Then we helped them aboard. At first a wounded man was put across.

'Where is your machinery?' I asked.

'Sunk,' said a Flight Sergeant.

'Any of the crew missing?'

'Yes, sir, the Captain.'

'Why?'

'Dead.'

Full speed ahead,' I commanded, for we had to get away quickly as the flare the men had lit could attract the enemy.

My men assisted the wounded man through the conning tower hatch. He was quite a young lad and looked pale and exhausted.

The other two Flight Sergeants followed behind. There was much activity below. The wounded flyer was lying in the chief engineer's bunk and five men were trying to undress him. The other two were sitting on a bunk surrounded by members of the crew who bombarded them with questions and supplied them with tea, chocolate, and cigarettes.

I could not believe my ears when I heard Walz, the cook, offer to make fried eggs for the airmen.

He usually guarded his eggs like a broody hen, snapping at everybody who dared so much as to hint at a desire for one. As I approached, the wounded boy tried to get up but I gently pushed him back again and examined his wounds. A bullet had grazed his shoulder and another had passed through his calf. They were clean flesh wounds which threatened no complications. During my examination I got him to tell us what had happened so as to distract his attention.

'Right over the ditch we encountered a British fighter, a Bristol Blenheim. He attacked us and combed us with his machine gun fire. We returned the fire and then the engineer cried out that we had been hit in the cooling system and we would have to get down. The English plane turned and was coming straight at us again. Our Captain crawled into the machine gun turret to return the fire. Suddenly the windscreen turned blood red and the pilot cried out, "I can't see". The next moment we were in the sea. We were all OK, only the Captain was dead. He had been hit through the head and the slip-stream had sent his blood against the windscreen. We pulled him in and all the time the English plane circled above us like a hawk. Every time he saw one of us he fired. That is how I got these two here. Finally we pushed our dead Captain out on to the wing of the plane and got out our dingy.

Then the English plane stopped firing at us, the dirty dog.

We had a pocket compass with us and started to paddle away eastward. The English plane circled around us for a while and then a second Bristol came towards us and flew close over us. They didn't shoot but they didn't try to save us either. We paddled all day and all night and then another night, forty hours altogether. We took it in turns, paddle for one hour, steer for one hour and sleep for one hour. There wasn't such a lot of sleep either. From time to time we fired our Véry light and then we saw you approaching. At first we thought you were English but when we heard you speak German we just simply went mad with joy.' He stopped.

I finished bandaging him.

'Well, that's all over now,' I said, 'first of all you must eat and then you can have a good long sleep.'

After the three had been fed they were put into bunks to sleep. I sent out a radio message, 'Airmen picked up, continuing course.'

I did not see my guests again until the next morning. The two sergeants stood about and looked longingly at the little round bit of sky which showed through the conning tower hatch. They seemed like birds in a cage, so I allocated them to the bridge watch so that from time to time they could get some fresh air.

We had hoped that the rescue of the airmen would be a good omen but it was as if from that hour we had taken a Jonah on board, for we did not sight a single objective. It was ideal weather with the sun shining in a cloudless sky and the sea gently undulating. Although it remained light long after sunset we saw nothing but sky and water and the horizon remained empty. For eleven days we cruised about in an area which was looked upon as one of the best hunting grounds. Nerves were stretched to breaking point. Glasses were glued to the eyes as we watched from the bridge and scanned the horizon. Nothing was to be seen, no smoke, no masts, no sails.

'Gradually we got into a mood which can only be compared to polar sickness. The least provocation would lead to flaring tempers and brawls. If the relief on the bridge arrived two minutes' late there was a devil of a fuss. Even the customary 'Keep your eyes skinned,' stuck in my throat whenever I left the bridge.

As we were doing our trim dive at dawn on the twelfth day, I was standing at the periscope and called over to Bohm, 'Gustav, your bloody periscope is covered in muck again.'

'But I've cleaned it, sir.'

At the same instant I caught sight of a steamer. It was like an electric shock.

'Action stations,' I shouted.

We rapidly approached the solitary tanker of about six thousand tons that was trying to evade us by zig-zagging wildly.

We dived underneath him and came up close astern. 'Prepare guns for firing,' I called.

I happened to turn round and the blood froze in my veins. Over on the west horizon a forest of masts had appeared. It was a large convoy. We dived immediately.

We had very nearly been caught in a U-Boat trap, for the single vessel had been sent on alone as a decoy, but I decided to go for the convoy.

For three hours we followed the convoy with the intention of cutting it off and coming to meet it. But it was hopeless, for underwater we were far too slow. When we surfaced again the forest of masts was floating far away on the horizon. Only a trawler was coming towards us with a foaming bow wave. We dived again and surfaced once more. This time a Sunderland came out of the clouds down at us so that we had to submerge quickly to take cover beneath the water.

By this time the convoy had disappeared. I cursed our luck as I looked through the periscope, but suddenly I noticed a steamer leisurely approaching us. It had apparently dropped out of the convoy. I estimated it at about six thousand tons.

The deck was laden with huge crates and on the fo'c'sle I counted eight guns.

We dived and sent him a torpedo which hit him amidships. Through the periscope I watched the crew take to the boats. Then the steamer slowly vanished in a foam. As we turned away we could still see the crates bobbing about in the water.

I saw through the slats in the crates that they contained aeroplane parts, wings, propellers and so on. We watched them sink one by one.

'There goes a flock of birds that will never fly,' said Meyer with satisfaction.

Now I thought that the spell had been broken but, ill-luck stayed with us and for the next seven days we saw nothing but sky and water.

The polar sickness on board assumed epidemic proportions. We couldn't stand the sight of each other any more and to see anyone eat or clean his teeth was enough to make one vomit.

On the seventh day the watch on the tower sang out, 'Steamer in sight.' It was a convoy again which one of the airmen had spotted. There were about thirty ships which appeared in a long line over the horizon.

As we were lying in an unfavourable position I let the convoy pass, came up astern of it and circled it in a wide sweep. It was evening before we made contact again, but this time we were well placed.

They made a lovely silhouette against the evening sky. I chose the three biggest ones, a tanker of twelve thousand tons, another of seven thousand tons and a third, a freighter, of seven thousand tons. We approached them underwater. I glued myself to the periscope and watched while the First Officer relayed my commands. Tube one was discharged, followed by tube two and a few seconds later tube three should have fired also. But tube three did not fire. From forrard came the sound of argument but just then I could not bother about it. I observed the effect of the explosion The first hit the *Cadillac,* the twelve thousand tonner.

There came the dull thud of the detonation, the up-spout of the water and behind it appeared the ship enveloped in yellow-brown smoke.

The second hit. I could hardly believe my eyes. It was a steamer we had not aimed at. The *Gracia* of five thousand six hundred tons. Immediately after came the freighter of seven thousand tons.

All three ships had been well and truly hit and not one of them could be saved.

We pushed off as fast as we could, while behind us depth charges stirred up the sea in our wake.

I sent for the torpedo man, 'What the hell happened just now? Why didn't you fire on my command?' He looked sheepish and said, 'I am sorry, sir, I slipped and fell on the hand-trigger and the torpedo went off too soon.'

I had to laugh. 'Well, anyhow, at least you hit something with it, but still you did us out of fourteen hundred tons.'

He was silent for a moment then he asked, 'How much was it altogether, sir?'

'Twenty-four thousand tons,' I said.

The news swept through the boat and faces shone like the sky after a long spell of rain.

At last our luck had changed. Two nights later we spotted a blacked-out steamer loaded with wheat; about two thousand eight hundred tons. In order to conserve torpedoes I made the crew take to their boats and sank the vessel with shells. We were fairly far from land and I followed the lifeboats and gave them bread, sausages and rum.

The following day brought us two ships. At the crack of dawn we got a four thousand tonner with a cargo of timber which we dispatched with a few shells below the water line. In the late afternoon we met a Dutch tanker loaded with diesel oil. On his bridge he carried a huge barrier of sandbags.

We gave him a few pounds from our 88, but instead of sinking the ship rose higher and higher in the water, with the oil draining into the sea the ship became more buoyant.

Finally we aimed our gun at his engine room and at last the ship began to sink. The lifeboats and the crew were already some distance away when we spotted three men floating in the water. They were the Third and Fourth Engineer and the Stoker. Their Captain had not bothered about them but had left them to drown in the engine room. I picked them up and followed the lifeboats and handed them over. Then I addressed a short speech to this Christian Captain beginning: 'You bloody bastard,' and ending in similar strain.

By now we had accounted for nearly forty thousand tons on this war patrol. Thirty-nine thousand, and eighty-five tons to be precise. We were beginning to be pleased with ourselves. But then we received a radio message, 'German U-Boat just returned from war patrol has sunk fifty-four thousand tons.' Her commander had been trained by us.

My men made long faces and Steinhagen, our sparks, gave

expression to the general opinion. 'It is annoying to see these young upstarts leave us standing.'

His chagrin struck me as rather childish but all the same I was glad to see the spirit of the crew under this provocation.

I called for the First and Second Officers. The result of our discussion was devastating, we had only six rounds of high explosive and a few torpedoes left. The following night we shot one of the torpedoes into the blue. A steamer went past us in the distance at considerable speed and we had to shoot quickly if we were to get her at all. When the torpedo had left the tube we began to count. First to fifty seconds…every second more made a hit all the more improbable.

One minute…one minute twenty…'My beautiful torpedo,' moaned Barendorff between set lips. We took up the chase but the steamer eluded us and darkness swallowed it up.

I was awakened with the news that the First Officer had spotted the *Empire Tucan,* a liner of seven thousand tons.

Our boat was rolling heavily in the swell. 'We shall have to attack her with shells,' I said. 'I don't know whether we can hit her in this sea,' remarked the First Officer.

I shrugged my shoulders. 'In any case we shall have to be even more sparing with our torpedoes.'

The bo'sun Meyer was called to lay the gun. He refused to come. 'To shoot in this weather is mad,' he told the man who woke him. 'There is far too much swell to take proper aim.'

We sent the runner a second time with a formal order from the bridge. Finally he turned up, sleepy and annoyed. I gave him my instructions. 'Your first shot will be on the guns which you can see clearly on the quarterdeck and your second will hit the bridge so that he can't radio.'

'Very good, sir,' he said, clicking his heels. But to judge by his expression he thought that we should economise with our shells as well. We stood on the bridge and observed the fire, for it was the last of our ammunition. The first shell hit the ship exactly between the guns and the second went into the fo'c'sle and the third into the stern, the fourth missed the target, the fifth was a dud and the sixth at last hit the bridge and was caught in the windsail. It was a weird sight. The pressure of the detonation within the sail pushed up what looked like a huge white ghost in the dawn and threw it right over the mast In spite of the last hit, the radio was operating furiously and sent out its SOS. The crew manned the boats and drew away from the ship. Only the wireless operator remained behind and continued sending messages.

There was nothing else we could do! We had to sacrifice a torpedo if we did not want to have the whole mob at our heels. The *Empire Tucan* was hit exactly amidships. The ship broke, dipped deep into the sea and then reared up again against the skyline. The operator was still at his station.

Suddenly we saw a man run across the sloping deck. He grasped a red lamp in his hand and holding it high above his head he leaped from the sinking ship. As he struck the water the red light went out. We stopped at the place where he had disappeared but we could not find him. Then shadows appeared in the north, dark shapes in the dusk, probably destroyers. As we had only one useable torpedo left we decided to push off. Three minutes later Steinhagen brought me a radio message. It was the last message of the *Empire Tucan. Torpedoed by U-boat sinking fast – SOS* and then a long dash…It was the operator's last signal.

The next ship we encountered two days later during our lunch hour. It was a Greek freighter which we finished off with our last torpedo. It was only four thousand tons.

Steinhagen put his head through the door. 'Have we got enough sir?' he asked breathlessly.

I had been counting already.

'No.' I said. 'We have fifty-one thousand tons and the other U-Boat has got three thousand tons more.'

A wave of disappointment swept through the boat. We began our return journey with one defective torpedo left on board.

I called the torpedoman, 'Have one more shot at getting the torpedo in order,' I told him.

The following morning he reported that the torpedo was in working order.

It was a clear and calm summer morning. We were steaming along in the vicinity of the coast in a calm sea. The lookout reported, 'A steamer on starboard bow.' A huge vessel with two funnels approached us out of the sun in wild zig-zags. Against the light it was impossible to determine her colour, but by her silhouette I recognised that it was a ship of the *Ormonde* class; that meant over fifteen thousand tons. 'Fellows,' I said and I felt their excitement. Cross your fingers and let's try and get it.' Then the command, 'Fire.'

'Then we waited, counting. Painfully slowly the seconds slipped by. The ship was a great distance away, too great a distance I feared. Then suddenly right amidship a column of water rose up far beyond the mast and immediately after we heard the crash of the detonation.

The liner heeled to starboard. In great haste lifeboats were launched, many of them. In between them hundreds of heads were bobbing in the water. It was not possible to help them because the coast was too close and the ship still afloat. On her fo'c'sle a number of guns were clearly visible. We retreated underwater. When a few minutes later we surfaced only the lifeboats were visible on calm sea.

I descended to my hole to make up the war diary.

As I passed the control-room I caught sight of a board which hung on the door on which was written:

66,587 tons,
Learn by heart.

Twelve
Scapa Flow

After dinner we stood about chatting in the mess of our depot ship. An orderly opened the door and Captain von Friedeburg entered. 'Gentlemen, your attention please. Corvette Captain Sobe and Captain Lieutenants Wellmer and Prien are requested to report to the CO U-Boats.' He saluted and left.

We looked at each other and my Commanding Officer asked me, 'What on earth is going on? What have you been up to? Have you been in a brawl or something?' He looked first at Wellmer and then at me. Wellmer answered for both of us. 'No, sir.' Ten minutes later we boarded a barge which was secured alongside and went over to the Weichsel. The harbour was peacefully quiet and we were silent too.

I considered what the CO could want with us, for such a command is most unusual on a Sunday. My companions were also lost in thought.

When we arrived on the Weichsel the crew of a U-Boat paraded on the *Tirpitz Mole*; the Commodore was inspecting them.

We went into the mess and waited. The minutes seemed liked hours, until finally a runner came. Clicking his heels he said, 'Will the Captains please go to the CO of the U-Boats in the Admiral's mess.'

Sobe went first and was followed by Wellmer. I remained alone and slipping up to the window gazed outside. What on earth was coming now I wondered. The thought was becoming unbearable.

At last the runner returned. 'Will Captain Prien please go to the

CO.' The runner preceded me up a few stairs and then I entered the large room. In the centre stood a large table covered with charts. Behind it stood the CO Wellmer and Sobe.

'Beg to report present.'

'Thank you, Prien,' the CO shook my hand.

'Now please listen carefully to Wellmer,' he said.

He turned to Wellmer. 'Wellmer, will you please begin from the beginning again.'

Wellmer stepped up to the table and bent over charts.

'The usual security measures are the same as always. The *particular* security measures which I reported in the war diary are at these points.' He placed his finger several places on the charts.

I followed him with my eyes. He was pointing at the Orkneys and in the centre of the charts was written in large letters *Bay of Scapa Flow.*

Wellmer explained further, but at that moment I could hardly follow him, for my thoughts were milling round the name Scapa Flow. Then Commodore Dönitz, U-Boat Commander, who was in the group said, 'During the Great War the British defence booms lay here.' He leaned over the chart and indicated the places with the point of a compass.

'In all probability they will be there again. In this place Emsmann was destroyed.' The compass point rested on Hoxa Sound.

'And here,' a stroke with the compass, 'are the usual anchorages of the British Fleet. All seven inlets of the bay will be boomed and well guarded. All the same I think that a resolute Commander could get through just here.' The point of the compass wandered over the chart. 'Mind you, it won't be an easy job because between the islands the current is very strong. All the same, I believe it can be done.'

He raised his head and gazed at me searchingly under lowered brows.

'What is your opinion, Prien?'

I stared at the chart, but before I could answer the CO continued.

'I don't want your answer now; think the matter over carefully, take all available information with you and study your chances. I shall expect your decision on Tuesday.' I straightened up and he looked me in the eyes. 'I hope that you have understood me, Prien. You are perfectly free to make your own decision. If you come to the conclusion that the understanding is impossible you will report that fact to me.' He continued emphatically, 'No blame whatsoever will be attached to you, Prien, because we know that your decision will be based on your own honest conviction.'

He shook me by the hand and I gathered up the charts and notes, saluted and left. I had myself taken out to the Depot ship *Hamburg*. I locked the charts and notes away in a steel safe and then I went home.

On the way soldiers and sailors saluted me but I returned their salutes mechanically. I felt a tremendous tension within me. Would it be possible to bring it off? My common sense calculated and questioned the chances, but my will had already decided that it could be brought off. At home, supper was already on the table. Absentmindedly I greeted my wife and child, for my thoughts were obsessed with the single idea of Scapa Flow. After supper I begged my wife to go out alone for I still had work to do. She nodded, smiling a little sadly. 'Oh yes, your next patrol.' But she left without further comment or question, for she was a soldier's daughter.

As soon as she had left I returned to the Depot ship *Hamburg*. I fetched the charts and the notes from the safe and took them home with me. Then I sat down at my writing table and spread the charts and plans out before me. I worked through the whole thing like a mathematical problem. The care with which the defences had been planned was amazing. By the time I had finished it was already dark. Bunching the papers together I took them back to the *Hamburg,* through the dark and silent town. Only the stars glowed clear in the sky.

Next morning I requested an interview with Captain van Friedeburg. He received me at once. 'Well,' he said, looking at me through narrowed eyes, 'What do you think, Prien?'

'When may I report to the CO, sir?' I asked.

'So you are going?'

'Yes, sir.'

He dropped heavily into his chair and reached for the telephone. 'I thought you might,' he said, 'only I wasn't sure on account of your wife and child.' Then he spoke into the telephone, 'Yes, sir, Prien is with me now...very good, sir... at 14 hours, sir.' He stood up.

'Two o'clock this afternoon you may see the CO' he said. 'The big lion is waiting,' he added.

Punctually at two I was there. As I entered I found him at his desk.

'Beg to report present, sir,' I said.

He did not acknowledge my salute; it seemed as if he hadn't noticed it. He was looking at me fixedly and asked. 'Yes or no?'

'Yes, sir.'

The shadow of a smile flitted across his face. Then seriously again he asked: 'Have you thoroughly considered the whole business? Did you think of Emsmann and Hennen?'

'Yes, I did, sir.' I replied.

'Very well, get your boat ready,' he said, 'We will fix the time of departure later on.' He got up, walked round the desk and shook my hand. He said nothing but his handshake was firm.

We left on October the eighth at ten o'clock in the morning. It was again a beautiful clear Sunday. Captain von Friedeburg stood on the pier with the adjutant of the Chief of the Flotilla. For a short while I stood with them on the wall looking over to the little boat which was made fast to the stakes. The crew was already on board.

We were walking up and down the pier hardly saying a word. Only right at the end Friedeburg said, 'Well, Prien, whatever happens you are sure of many thousands of tons – and now – the best of luck, my boy.'

I saluted and walked across the gangway to the boat.

The ropes were cast off and the roar of the diesels thundered through the boat. Then we were slowly making for the grey green sea, our course nor'nor'west and our objective *Scapa Flow*.

The two figures on shore faded into the pale grey haze. The land sunk behind the horizon and then there was only the sky and the sea, green and chilled by the autumn. A tired sun shed pale light over the water.

Course nor'nor'west. No one on board knew the objective, only I. We sighted a fishing trawler and submerged. We sighted the smoke threads of distant ships beyond the horizon but we did not give chase. The crew looked at me questioningly but nobody said a thing and I could not speak. It was hard to keep silent before such shipmates.

The weather that had been sunny on the first day gradually got worse, as we sailed into a depression which came over from Ireland. The wind increased in strength and the watch on the bridge had to don oilskins. On the heights of Duncranby Head the barometer fell. The wind freshened to gale force.

Seas rose up, dark, menacing and foam-capped, and the wave-tops gleamed palely through the evening grey sky. We stood on the tower and our eyes tried to pierce the dimness. There was nothing. There were no stars, for the sky was overhung with heavy clouds from which came an incessant drizzle. There were no lights, for war had switched them off with one gesture. Only darkness was around me. On the port a shadow could be seen over the waves.

The islands.

We were nearing our objective, we were moving near to the enemy.

Endrass leaned toward me, 'Are we going to visit the Orkneys, sir?'

The time had come when I could speak.

'Take hold of yourself,' I said, 'we are going Scapa Flow.'

I could not see his face. The wind was blowing and the water roared. And then his quiet and firm voice came through the noise, 'That will be OK sir, that will be quite OK.'

'Endrass,' I thought, 'you couldn't have said anything better at this moment,' but all I said was, 'We will lie off the coast on the bottom. Tell the crew to assemble in the forrard mess.'

The shadowy coast dropped below the horizon and we were alone between sky and water. Half an hour later we closed the conning tower hatch. The deep hum of the vents echoed through the ship. The water ran noisily into the tanks as we dived.

The howling of the wind faded and the sea became calm, for we were sinking into the silence of the deep. There was only the high-pitched whine of the electric motors, then a barely perceptible shock, and the motors were cut. We were lying on the bottom.

It was October the 13th and it was four o'clock in the morning.

I made my way to the forrard mess. The men were already there, and stood against the walls or crouched in the bunks. The glare of the unshaded lamps made their faces look chalky white, with deep black smudges for eyes.

'Tomorrow we shall enter Scapa Flow,' I said without any introduction.

There was a silence so profound that I could hear water dripping somewhere, clop...clop...clop...

'Everyone except the watch will go to their bunks and sleep, the watch will wake the cook at 14.00 hours. At 16.00 hours we will have dinner. Then for the duration of the mission there will be no more hot food. Only cold sandwiches at all stations. And everyone will have a slab of chocolate. All superfluous light will be extinguished, we must economise on current; no one is to move unnecessarily, for we shall be lying aground for this evening and must be careful with the air. During the mission itself there must be absolute silence. No message is to be repeated, do you understand?'

'Yes sir,' they said as one man.

'Crew dismiss.'

Silence. They were crouching on their bunks and looking at me. Their faces were quite calm and nothing was to be read in them, neither astonishment, nor fear.

I went aft to my hutch and lay down. Overhead was the white-painted shell of the boat from which a few rivet heads looked blindly down at me.

The lights were doused one after the other, till the boat was in almost total darkness. There was an uncanny silence; only now and then the sea gurgled against the sides of the boat. In the control room the watch were holding a whispered conversation.

I thought of the men lying in their bunks forrard.

They had all been with me long enough to know what tomorrow's mission signified. But not a single one of them had betrayed his thoughts. They had kept silent and if in this hour any one of them had to sort something out in his mind, he did it quietly and without words.

I would like to have slept but could not. I closed my eyes and the chart of Scapa Flow appeared in my mind's eye. *The Bay with the Seven Inlets through one of which I had to pass.* I tried to imagine my path.

At last I could not stick it any longer. On tip-toe I crept through the boat. The long half-dark room was filled with a curious unrest. There was a rasping of throats and a heavy turn in the bunks here and there, and a few of the men raised their heads as I passed.

In the ward-room I found Spahr, my tall navigator, bending over the charts.

'You here?'

'Sir, I had to look at the chart once more,' he said in excuse. We stood side by side and stared at the chart. Then Spahr whispered, 'Do you believe, sir, that we can get in?'

'Do you think that I am a prophet, Spahr?'

'And suppose it goes wrong?'

'Well, then we will have had very bad luck,'

The curtain in front of one of the bunks rustled back and Endrass poked out his head.

'I can't sleep any more, sir, and you can court-martial me if you like,' he said.

'Shut up and save the air;' I hissed at him. With a sigh he subsided in his hole.

I crept back to my bunk and lay down again. This time I succeeded in falling asleep, but it was a very light sleep with one eye open.

At 14.00 hours I heard the watch wake the cook and saw him creep past through half-closed eyes.

He had wrapped his feet in rags to avoid making any noise, for the hearing apparatus of the enemy was very sensitive. In some circumstances it was possible to hear the tread of a boot on the iron-floor plates in the next ship.

At 16.00 hours we were all awakened. The meal consisted of veal cutlets and green cabbage. It was a feast and the orderlies were kept on the run. I sat with Wessels and Barendorff. The latter kept us entertained. He was as lively as a cricket.

The tables were cleared. Three men went through the boat and fixed the charges with which to blow up the ship in case we should fall into the hands of the enemy.

Once more I went through all rooms and gave my final instructions. During the whole of the action no one was to smoke and even more important no one was to speak unnecessarily. The last preparations were made. Everyone inspected his life jacket. I cast a last glance at the escape hatch. The navigator fixed his chart.

Those of us who were going on the bridge put on oil-skins.

19.00 hours. It would be night outside. Brief commands, 'Diving stations,' and then, 'Get in trim.' The bilge pumps began to work and Wessels, the chief engineer, reported: 'Boat rising… 1 metre up, 2 metres up.'

The whine of the motors started up and the boat began to surface. I went to the control-room.

'Up periscope'; slowly and cautiously the tube rose and its glassy eye scanned the horizon. It was night.

I took a deep breath and ordered, 'Surface'.

Compressed air streamed into the tanks from which the water rushed gurgling. 'Down periscope', and the tube sank back into the boat. And then came the noise when the boat breaks surface, rocking as if half drunk from the immersion. With a dull thud the hatch opened. A current of fresh air streamed in and we climbed out as fast as we could, the two officers, the Bo'sun and myself.

Straining my ears I listened in the darkness. There was nothing to hear and nothing to see. The wind had dropped and there was a slight swell. I looked around and the others reported half aloud and yet quite clearly. 'Starboard clear!'…'Port clear!'…'Aft clear!'

'Ventilate the boat,' I commanded and the two fans began to spin.

'Both diesels?' and from below, 'Both diesels are ready.'

'Stop electric motors! Both diesels slow ahead.'

The familiar hum of the engines began and with a spreading bow wave the boat moved forward.

By now our eyes had become accustomed to the night and we could see everything clearly – almost too clearly. The boat, the approaching waves and behind them – the coastline.

'It's curiously light tonight,' I said.

'I can't imagine why, sir,' answered Endrass.

There was a strange brightness which came neither from the moon nor from a searchlight. Its source was hidden. It seemed as if in the north, behind the horizon, bonfires were illuminating the cloud bank. Like a blow it struck me. The Northern Lights! No one had thought of that! We had selected the night of the new moon for the enterprise and now it was becoming lighter every moment, for the north wind was slowly pushing the cloud bank aside.

I asked myself whether I should submerge once more and wait for the following night, for in these latitudes the Northern Lights are rarely seen twice running. I turned round. With his glasses to his eyes Endrass was staring across the sea to port.

'Well, what is it?' I asked.

'Well, sir, it is a good light for shooting,' he said quietly, and at the same time I heard Barendorff whisper to the signaller:

'Man, it's going to be a sticky night, tonight.'

I wondered whether my lads would be in the same mood on the following day.

Then I ordered the new course. 'Both engines half-speed ahead.'

The bow wave increased and threads of spume were flung across the deck.

We gazed into the night.

It's curious how responsibility sharpens one's faculties. A long way in front of us a shadow lay on the water, too dim to be properly seen through the glasses. Perhaps it was a fishing smack, perhaps a neutral steamer passing in the distance. But in our situation every encounter threatened danger. 'Alarm: Diving stations.'

We scuttled through the hatch into the boat. 'Flood tanks,' and water poured into the tanks. 'Up periscope.' I rushed to the periscope and searched for the vessels. From below came Number One's voice giving orders to the planesman, and then came Spahr'a deep and calm voice, 'To the commander, time to alter course, 20 degrees to starboard.'

'Starboard 15,' I called back.

After a short pause the planesman answered, 'Steady on new course.' Up above the shadow had disappeared. On the other hand the north wind had pushed the compact bank of clouds over to the south, only a thin veil of mist was trailing behind them across the sky. But in this veil the Northern Lights showed brighter than ever, shooting orange and blue rays to the zenith of the heavens. A magic light as on the Day of Judgment.

We had approached closer to the land. The hills had become more solid and their silhouettes showed black and sombre against the bright sky. Their shadows fell dark and hard over the pale and gleaming water.

'Sir, have you seen the Northern Lights?' said a calm and rather oily voice behind me. 'I have never seen anything like it.'

I turned round. 'Man...' I started to curse, but immediately I became silent again when I saw Samann. There he stood, his eyes wide open like a child's listening to a fairy tale. And yet he knew as well as I what was at stake. Wordlessly I turned back again. The shadows of the hills right and left merged together and the water darkened. For the glow in the sky had vanished.

And then suddenly it was light again. A bay opened out in front of us far into the horizon, in which the burning sky was mirrored. It was as if the sea was illuminated from below.

'We are inside,' I said.

There was no reply, but it seemed to me as if the whole boat was holding its breath, and as if the hearts of the motors were beating quieter and faster.

It was a wide bay. Although the hills which surrounded it were very high, from the boat they looked like a low chain of dunes. Cautiously peering in all directions we moved forward into the still water.

A few lights over the water flared up like shooting stars. I felt the blood hammer in my temples. But they were only tankers, sleeping at anchor.

At last over there…close to the shore appeared the mighty silhouette of a battleship. Hard and clear, as if painted into the sky with black ink. The bridge, the mighty funnel and aft, like filigree, the tall mast. Slowly we edged closer. At such a moment all feeling stopped. One became part of the boat, the brain of this steel animal which was creeping up towards its enormous prey. At such a time you must think in iron and steel – or perish.

We crept closer still. Now we could clearly see the bulge of the gun turrets, out of which the guns jutted threateningly into the sky. The ship lay there like a sleeping giant.

I believe she belongs to the *Royal Oak* class,' I whispered, and Endrass nodded silently.

We crept closer still and suddenly behind the first silhouette loomed up the outlines of a second battleship as large and as powerful as the first. We could recognise her superstructures behind the stern of the *Royal Oak;* the bridge and the forrard gun turret.

It was the *Repulse.*

We had to attack her first, for the *Royal Oak,* right in front of us, was a certainty, anyhow.

'All tubes ready.'

The command echoed below in the boat. Then silence, but for the gurgling sound when water ran into the tubes; a sharp hiss of compressed air followed and then a hard metallic click when the lever snapped into position.

Then came back the report, 'Tube one ready.'

'Tube fire,' commanded Endrass.

A thud trembled through the boat; the torpedo was on its way. If only it would hit – it had to hit – for the silhouette had been right in the centre of the sights

And now Spahr's dark voice was counting, 5, 10, 15. Time became eternity. There wasn't a sound in the boat, only Spahr's voice dropping heavily into the stillness. 20. Our eyes were fixed on the target but still the steel fortress remained unmoved. Suddenly at the bows of the *Repulse* a column of water spouted into the air and immediately after it the dull detonation reached us. It sounded rather like blasting in a distant quarry.

'He's got his,' said Endrass.

I had no reply but, 'Second tube ready?'

I manoeuvred the boat towards the *Royal Oak*. We had to be quick about it otherwise they would be in our hair before we let go the second torpedo.

'Port 5,' the boat turned slowly to port.

'Midships. Wheel's amidships.' We were pointing straight at the *Royal Oak*. She grew mightier than ever. Her shadow seemed to come to reach out at us. Schmidt was steering as though he could see the target himself. The thread of the sights cut directly amidships,

Now was the moment. 'Tube, fire,' commanded Endrass.

Again the recoil shuddered and again Spahr's voice began to count. '5…10…'

But now something occurred that no one had anticipated and no one who had seen it would ever forget. A wall of water shot up toward the sky. It was as if the sea suddenly stood up on end. Loud explosions came one after the other like drumfire in a battle and coalesced into one mighty ear-splitting crash

Flames shot skyward, blue…yellow…red.

Behind this hellish firework display the sky disappeared entirely. Like huge birds, black shadows soared through the flames, fell hissing and splashing into the water. Fountains yards high sprang up where they had fallen, huge fragments of the mast and the funnels.

We must have hit the munition magazine and the deadly cargo had torn the body of its own ship apart.

I could not take my eyes from the glass. It was as if the gates of hell had suddenly been torn open and I was looking into the flaming furnace. I glanced down into my boat.

Down there it was dark and still I could hear the hum of the motors, Spahr's even voice and the answers of the planesman. I felt as never before my kinship with these men below who did their duty silently and blindly, who could neither see the day nor the target and who died in the dark if it had to be.

I called down, 'He's finished.'

For a moment there was silence. Then a mighty roar went through the ship, an almost bestial roar in which the pent-up tension of the past twenty-four hours found release.

'Silence!' I shouted…and the ship became quiet. Only Spar's voice was heard. 'Three points to port,' and the planesman's answering, 'Three points to port.'

Over the *Royal Oak* the fireworks died down, revived for a short while by an occasional belated explosion. The bay awoke to feverish authority. Searchlights flashed and probed with their long white fingers over the water and died.

Lights were flitting here and there…small swift lights low over the water, the lights of destroyers and U-Boat chasers. Like dragonflies they zig-zagged over the dark surface. If they caught us we were done for.

I took a last look round. The stricken ship was dying. I could see no other worthwhile target, only pursuers.

'Hard aport,' I ordered, 'Both engines full speed ahead. There was only one thing to attempt now. Get out of this witches' cauldron and take the boat and the crew safely home.

The hills closed in again; the current, which here had the force of a raging torrent, took us in its grip and shook us from side to side. The engines were running flat out.

We seemed to advance at a snail's pace and at times even to be motionless like a trout in a mountain stream. Behind us the headlight of a destroyer detached itself from the welter of light and came streaming towards us. But we could not, *we could not* get ahead. The boat being tossed from side to side while the enemy was steadily gaining on us. Already we could make out its narrow silhouette against the sky.

'Wonder whether he'll get us?' said Endrass in a husky voice.

'Extreme speed ahead,' I called out.

'Engines are running at extreme speed,' came the reply.

'Couple up electric motors. Give us everything we've got.'

It was a nightmare. There we lay, held fast by visible power, while death came closer, ever closer.

A spot of light flashed dot-dash-dot.

'He is signalling,' whispered Endrass.

The boat shuddered as it strained against the current.

We must get out... *we must get out.* This single thought throbbed in my brain to the rhythm of the engines. *We must get out...*

Then – wonder of wonders – the pursuer turned aside. The light slid away over the water and then *weeyummm* of the first depth charges.

Laboriously, painfully, the boat wriggled through the narrows. It was dark again. From the distance came ever more faintly the thuds of the depth charges

Before us lay the sea, broad and free, vast under the limitless sky.

Taking a deep breath I turned to give the final command of this action.

'All stations. Attention. One battleship destroyed, one battleship damaged – and we are through!'

This time I allowed them to roar.

Thirteen

Audience With Hitler

Everything went on as before. Watches were set, we ate and drank and slept as always. But our nerves were still tingling with the excitement of the past. Next midday, when we were already far away in the North Sea radio announced:

> *The British battleship* Royal Oak *was attacked and sank by a German U-Boat in the bay of Scapa Flow. According to British messages the U-Boat was also sank.*

I happened to be in the control-room when the announcement came through. Beside me stood Bohm. We looked at each other. Suddenly he burst out with a roar of laughter; 'So we're sunk, eh? Now ain't that just too bad? Ain't we the poor bloody bastards?'

What had to be done had been done, but the thrill of the exploit remained with us for a long time.

The third morning we sighted land, a thin blue line above the waves. Soon the mole stretched a long stone arm out to us in welcome across the sea. Hansel, the signaller reported breathlessly: 'Sir, semaphore signal just received. Admiral is awaiting boat at the lock.'

'Thank you,' I acknowledged, pleased and embarrassed at the same time, and ordered the crew to parade on deck.

As we approached the military band raised their glittering instruments and struck up the anthem. A large crowd of people cheered and waved as we passed through the lock and made fast. As I stepped from the bridge gangway on to the quay and approached the man in the blue greatcoat, the solemnity of the hour all but overwhelmed me.

My throat was tight and dry as I made my report: 'Beg to report boat returned from mission. One enemy battleship sunk, one damaged.'

The Admiral thanked me in the name of the Führer and the Navy. Then the others came up and shook my hand, beginning with Rear-Admiral Dönitz, commander of the U-Boat flotilla. *Why the thanks? Yours was the head and mine merely the hand that carried it out.* But the presence of the others kept me silent.

We left the lock and went to our permanent berth in the harbour. Hardly had we tied up when an officer came on board and handed me an invitation from the Führer to go to Berlin. Commander and crew were to be his guests at the Chancellery.

Then followed the flight to Berlin in the Führer's own plane the landing at the Tempelhof, the triumphal drive through cheering crowds of ten of thousands of people who were lining the streets.

We arrived at the Chancellery. The crew paraded in the large study. From the street came the muted cheers of the crowd.

The adjutant entered and announced the Führer.

He came in. I had often seen him before, but never had I felt his greatness as intensely as in this moment. Certainly I stood here, too, thus realising a dream of my youth and the realization of one's youthful ambition is perhaps the best life has to offer. But what was I in comparison with this man, who had felt the degradation of this land on his own, who had dreamed of a freer and happier Fatherland! An unknown man among eighty millions he had dreamed and acted. His dream had come true, his acts had forged a new world.

I marched up to the Führer. He shook me by the hand and placed the Knight's Cross of the Iron Cross around my neck, honouring my whole crew through me.

I felt pride and happiness in this hour; it would be idle to deny it. But I knew that I stood here, a symbol for the many who, nameless and silent, had fought the same fight.

Success had singled me out. But what after all is success? A matter of luck, of providence? That which matters among men is to have the heart of a fighter and to lose one's self in the cause he serves.

The Führer walked along the short line of men, gave everyone his hand and thanked each one of them. I walked behind him and looked at every one of them, man for man, and my heart beat in unison with theirs.

Postscript

Berlin, 23 May 1941

The High Command of the Wehrmacht makes the following announcement:

The U-Boat commanded by Korvetten-Kapitän *Günther Prien has failed to return from its last war patrol. The vessel must be presumed lost.*

Korvetten-Kapitän Günther Prien, *the hero of Scapa Flow, was honoured by the Führer with the Oak Leaves to the Knight's Cross of the Iron Cross in recognition of his eminent services. He and his brave crew will live for ever in German hearts.*